Carlo Collodi, M. A. Murray

The Story of a Puppet

Or, The Adventures of Pinocchio

Carlo Collodi, M. A. Murray

The Story of a Puppet
Or, The Adventures of Pinocchio

ISBN/EAN: 9783337176709

Printed in Europe, USA, Canada, Australia, Japan

Cover: Foto ©ninafisch / pixelio.de

More available books at **www.hansebooks.com**

THE

ADVENTURES OF MARK WILLIS.

BY
MRS. GEORGE CUPPLES,
AUTHOR OF "THE STORY OF OUR DOLL," "THE LITTLE CAPTAIN,"
ETC. ETC.

LONDON:
T. NELSON AND SONS, PATERNOSTER ROW;
EDINBURGH; AND NEW YORK

1872.

Contents.

I. SETTING OUT IN LIFE,
II. FIRST DAYS AT SEA,
III. DOWN THE TROPICS,
IV. AFRICAN COAST-TRADE,
V. PRIVATE TRADERS,
VI. WATCHING THE SLAVER,
VII. CHINA,
VIII. HOMEWARD BOUND,

THE ADVENTURES OF MARK WILLIS.

CHAPTER I.

SETTING OUT IN LIFE.

"SAY, Mark," shouted a boy about thirteen years of age to another who was sitting under the shade of the noble lime-trees in the old 'College Green,' Bristol—"I say, are you not going with us to Clifton this afternoon?"

Mark sighed as he answered, "No, Bently, I can't go."

"Why, what's come over you, Mark?" replied his friend. "You were always ready to enjoy our half-holidays, and now you do nothing but sit here moping and making yourself miserable. Come along; I know your mother would like you to go,—she said to me this morning she hoped you would, at any rate."

"Oh yes, I know that; but I tell you I cannot come;"

and Mark rose up and walked away in the direction of his home, leaving Jack Bently standing staring at him.

"Well," he said, as he joined some other boys who were waiting for him, "I can't make the fellow out. He must have taken his father's death dreadfully to heart; or it may be because people say they are poor now, and will have to come down in the world. Well, it's a pity, whatever the reason is, for Mark was a good fellow."

When the boys were gone, Mark, who had only walked to the other side of the green, came back to his seat, and sat down once more with the same listless look about him. He pulled a book out of his pocket and began to read, but soon put it away again; and, leaning his back against one of the trees, he gazed through the entrance to the green at the masts of the ships, the flapping sails, and small craft plying about the river. He closed his eyes and listened to the strange medley of sounds: the busy hum of men; the rush of carriage wheels; the Heave-yo of the sailors as they warped a ship, newly arrived, to its berth; and to the swift run of the crane as it dropped its heavy burden with a dull thud into the hold. Above all came the sudden swell of the organ booming through the open door of the cathedral, and Mark opened his eyes to exclaim, "Oh, I wish 'old Fritz' would stop! We have enough of it every day, I'm sure; but he's practising, I suppose, some of his great pieces."

He drew the book again from his pocket and read very

steadily for some time, as long as the organ was played; but when the last notes had died away, Mark stopped too, and was preparing to go home in real earnest, when a cheery voice close to him said, "Why, how now! not away with the boys, Mark?"

"No, sir," said Mark, smiling, and sitting down again beside the new-comer; "I was listening to your music, Mr. Offenbach. I began by wishing you would stop; but it did me so much good, that I wished you would go on."

"That shows me there is something wrong here," said the organist, tapping Mark on the head with his cane; "or perhaps here," and he gave a sudden poke at his heart. "Come now, my boy," he continued, "let's have the trouble out."

Father Fritz, as the boys called him, was a German by birth; and though in reality not past the prime of life, he was so bald, so short and stout, that he looked quite old, and, especially when he had his spectacles on, quite venerable. He was so extremely good-natured that he was a great favourite with the boys employed as choristers, and it was quite a common thing for them to go with their troubles to him, for he was wonderfully clever at helping them out of a difficulty. It was distinctly understood among the boys that he was far more learned than the master, or even than the very bishop himself, for he could speak several, if not all, the languages, living and dead.

Mark turned slightly away from his kind friend and hung down his head, for somehow a tear had dropped into the corner of his eye, and he dared not raise his hand to rub it off. But Mr. Offenbach had seen it quite plainly; he saw everything, somehow, though he moved about so slowly, and always appeared to be in a perfect brown study. "The truth is, my dear boy," he said, gently putting his arm round the boy's neck, "I've observed you for several days. I am told you don't sing with the others, and I know it is true, for I miss your voice— and one of the best contraltos it is too, and of course it is missed easily. Now, there's something wrong. Come, Mark, I lost my father too. Yours was very fond of you, wasn't he?"

"Yes," said Mark, choking back a sob bravely; "but it isn't that—I mean, not altogether. Well, I *will* tell you, Mr. Fritz; you have helped me before now."

"That's right, my boy," was the reply; "I may *not* be able to help you, but a burden shared is easier carried."

Then Mark told how, by his father's death, he and his mother and two brothers were now left in very straitened circumstances, and how it was decided they were to live in a small house near the harbour, where his mother might be able to take in lodgers. What distressed Mark was, that he knew his mother was doing this for his sake, that he might attend school and get a good education. She had been advised to go into the country instead, where her limited means would keep her and the two little boys comfortably, and Mark might get a situation as junior clerk in some of the many warehouses in Bristol. But this she had distinctly refused to do, and had therefore lost many friends. "And now," said Mark, "after my mother has made her arrangements, and is beginning to get settled in her mind about it, I feel I cannot live this life any longer. I cannot let her work for me, and I must do something to give her back all the comforts she had before my father died."

"That is a right spirit, my boy," said Mr. Offenbach; "but what can a boy like you do? You must wait patiently, and when your education is finished, no doubt some of your father's friends will step forward to help you to a good situation."

"But I cannot wait," said Mark, impatiently. "I must do something now. I've thought it all over a hundred times, and it forces itself into my mind constantly. It nearly drives me mad to sit quietly there, day after day, at these weary lessons, or in the quiet, gloomy cathedral to sit singing, while I know my mother must work, she who never soiled a finger before, and all for me, to keep me chained down to school, and afterwards to a stool in an office. No; I must leave it all. I must be—"

Mark stopped suddenly, as if he were afraid to speak

out the words which would fix his position in life, or as if he had never brought his thoughts to so decided a termination.

"You must be what?" said Mr. Fritz. "Ah," he said, "I think I guess;" and he looked at the book Mark had been reading, but which had fallen on the grass, and as it lay open the organist saw it was a manuscript book and not a school-book, but had at the head of one of the pages the title, "Eminent Men of Bristol." "You want to follow in their steps," continued Mr. Fritz, laughing and rubbing his hands. "Who have we here?" and he began to read from the book. "'Sebastian Cabot, who sailed from this harbour in the *Matthew*, accompanied by other ships, on a voyage of discovery, and in the course of the same year touched Newfoundland—being the first person who ever set foot on the *mainland* of America. In returning home he sailed along the coast as far as Florida; and by virtue of this visit North America became annexed to the English Crown.' Very good," said Mr. Fritz; "I believe this said Cabot was the son of a Venetian, but born in Bristol, and to him England stands indebted for her magnificent possessions in the New World. But he was a man, you see, when he set out, and a rich one too. Well, well, let us turn to the next. 'Old Dampier, the gallant buccaneer, having sailed from Bristol, with two armed vessels, on an expedition in search of Spanish treasure-ships, anchored off the island of Juan Fernandez. Perceiving a light on shore during the night, he sent a boat to reconnoitre, which, not returning, the pinnace went in search; but soon came back from the shore with abundance of crayfish, and a *man clothed in goats' skins*, who looked more wild than their first owners. This man was Alexander Selkirk—the original of Robinson Crusoe—who was taken to Bristol after having been on the island four years and four months.'

"It all comes to this, I see," said Mr. Offenbach, shutting the book, "that you want to go to sea. You want to leave your mother alone to fight for herself; and, perhaps, break her heart to part with you, for you are her eldest child, I think. You want to become a great discoverer, or a buccaneer, or a man clothed in goats' skins. But, my boy, before you can be one or the other, you have a hard life before you. Think well of it, my boy. A sailor's life is the hardest life in the world."

"I *have* thought of it, Mr. Fritz. You are very severe upon me," said Mark, the tears standing in his eyes. "It is to help my mother I want to go. I don't mind the hard life; it's twice as hard living this quiet life here. I don't want to be a discoverer, or anything but a sailor; and by-and-by a captain of a ship, like my mother's brother, my uncle John."

Mr. Fritz sat thinking, quietly poking his cane into the grass at his feet, and whistling under his breath the first notes of a new symphony. Mark became impatient, and interrupted his reverie by saying, "Won't you help me, Mr. Fritz? Could you speak to my mother about it for me? I feel that I could do something. I'm sure I should get on and make money. I *will*," he ended, standing up suddenly with determination in his attitude.

"Well, I suppose somebody must do it," said Mr. Fritz, taking off his spectacles, and pulling out his watch. "Tell your mother I will do myself the honour of calling upon her this evening at six o'clock. It is a disagreeable task you have given me, Mark; but I may do it better than another, seeing I have a mother of my own, who was placed in similar circumstances. Not exactly: I did not go to sea, but my rock ahead was that great old organ in there," he said, laughing. Then he continued, "Remember, I'm a punctual man, Master Mark, as becomes the assistant organist of St. Augustine's. Goodbye till six o'clock."

Mark now went straight home, feeling as if a load had been lifted off his mind, and very much pleased to think it was lying on the shoulders of "Father Fritz" instead.

When he went into the parlour he found his mother sitting sewing. They were still in the old house where his father had died, but were to leave it in a few days for the humbler one close to the river; and Mark could not help shuddering when he looked round the comfortable room and thought of that other incongenial house, so dif-

MARK AND HIS MOTHER.

ferent from what they had been accustomed to. For some days Mark had been very silent and gloomy, but now he appeared quite different, as he came into the room, and announced that "Father Fritz" was coming at six o'clock. "You have never seen him, mamma," said Mark, a little excitedly; "but you will be sure to like him; he's awfully clever, and knows exactly how to advise you about anything that is troubling you."

Mrs. Willis did not ask why Mr. Offenbach was coming: she had a presentiment that her boy was making up his mind to take some decided step, but she never thought it was to take him from her altogether; still she was a little nervous about it, and kept her eyes fixed on her work, fearing to read the truth in her son's face. Fortunately the maid-servant came in with the dinner; and during the time it lasted, neither mother nor son spoke about the intended visit, but mutually avoided the subject.

As the clock was striking six, the loud rat-tat sounded on the knocker, and Mark hastened to meet the kind-hearted organist. "Shall I come in with you, sir?" said Mark, showing by his breathing how agitated he really was, and evidently was much relieved when Mr. Offenbach said, "Not at present, Mark; not for half an hour and five minutes." Mark could not help smiling, as he went to his own room, at "Father Fritz's" odd habit of being accurate to a moment; and also to see that he had on his blue spectacles, a sure sign he had some weighty business on his mind. It seemed a long half-hour; but punctually to the minute Mark was sent for, and he crept into the parlour like one guilty in spite of himself. He was surprised, however, to find his mother more composed than he could have believed possible, and he wondered how Mr. Fritz had managed to soothe her so effectually, but he could not ask then how the news had been broken. For a moment his mother's lip quivered, and she looked as if she were going to cry again, as she had evidently been doing before Mark entered, but she held out her hand to him and drew him close to her as she said, "Poor boy, it's a foolish step this, but I know it is from a sincere desire to help me. But will nothing induce you to give it up, my son?"

"O mother, please don't ask me!" said Mark, sobbing. "I can't live here now. I must get away from it all. I've long wanted to be a sailor. I would have been, even if papa had lived. I could never have gone into one of these hateful offices."

It was therefore all settled that Mark should go one voyage — Mr. Offenbach and his mother hoping that on his return he would have had enough of it, and would then settle down to his lessons once more. Mrs. Willis herself called upon the owners of her brother's ship, and was received very kinkly by the head of the firm, who promised to keep Mark's name in remembrance for the first ship of theirs that sailed. While they were waiting, Mrs. Willis removed to her new house, which was close to the river and harbour; and if Mark had been anxious to try the life of a sailor before, he was eager now. His bedroom window had a view of the river at the lower portion, called the "Welsh Back," toward the docks. There was always some vessel going out or coming in, with the usual exciting stir about the harbour and river's bank. And he often managed to get on board some of the vessels. One afternoon a ship anchored almost

THE "BLUE-BELL" AT HER MOORINGS.

opposite his very window, and he could lie in bed and see the men working aloft in the early summer mornings. The captain of the ship, the *Blue-Bell*, hearing that Mrs. Willis had two rooms to let, came on shore and took them for himself and his wife, who arrived the next day. Captain Walker was soon made acquainted with Mark's intentions, and the two became great friends, Mark spending every spare moment on board the *Blue-Bell*. There was every prospect that in the end he would sail in this ship, as no message had been sent from his uncle's firm; but one great objection to it was, it was a guano ship, bound for the Peruvian coast; and, by what he had heard some of the men saying, it was by no means a pleasant business. He greatly preferred the idea of going to the East Indies, or to China, where his uncle sailed to, though his mother did not like to contemplate such a long voyage as that. One morning, however, when Mark's patience was nearly exhausted, his mother received a letter from "Price and Co.," asking her to call with her son the next forenoon at their office. Accordingly, they set out together, Mark trying, but in vain, to hide his extreme pleasure before his mother. Mr. Price seemed to be pleased with Mark's appearance, and stated that he had been trying to get him a berth on board an Indiaman, but had not been successful. The only ship they had leaving port for some time was the *Stratton*, a large brig, going to the Canary Islands—"And," he added, as if by the way, "also bound for the Gaboon River."

"And where, may I ask, is the Gaboon River?" said Mrs. Willis.

"It's down the west coast, ma'am," said Mr. Price,

hurriedly, no doubt wishing to hide what precise coast he referred to. "We get palm oil, ivory, and sometimes gold dust thereabouts." Here the attention of Mr. Price was claimed by other visitors, on business of probably a more important nature. Mark and his mother therefore left as soon as the arrangement had been completed by their jointly signing an indenture as apprentice to the firm; this being done in the outer office, and duly witnessed, so as to bind either side to fulfil their engagement, under legal penalties.

That same evening, while Mrs. Willis sat busily at work upon Mark's clothes, he got his Atlas at her request, and looked up the exact whereabouts of the Gaboon River. "Here it is, mamma," said Mark, delightedly. "See, I sail all down the Atlantic Ocean, past France and Spain and Madeira, to the Canaries; then, after, past the Cape de Verds, and down the west coast of Africa to the Gaboon."

"The west coast of Africa, did you say, Mark?" said Mrs. Willis, in evident distress. "Why, that is a most unhealthy place; it is the very region of ague and fever. O my boy, I wish you had not persevered in this notion of yours."

"Nonsense, mamma," said Mark, cheerily. "It is a famous place to make money in. I mean to take some small looking-glasses, and some fine glass beads; I'm told I can exchange them with the natives for an elephant's tusk, or a cocoa-nut full of gold-dust, or something more valuable still. The steward of the *Blue-Bell* has been telling me all about it. He says they will even give pieces of gold for old bits of iron, and used-up hatchets, and red cotton handkerchiefs, but that the most valuable thing of all is an old brass kettle."

"If cotton handkerchiefs are so valuable as all that, Mark," said Mrs. Willis, smiling, "I think I must buy you some additional ones; they must be worth their weight in gold. But for all that, my boy, I tremble when I think of the danger you run from the climate."

"Here, Mark, take mine," said little Harry, tugging his small handkerchief out of his pocket. "Old iron, did you say? I know where to find an old horse-shoe; I'll run and fetch it."

"I'm sure we might give Mark the brass kettle that's in the kitchen; we could use the copper one," said Charles. "Shall we go and ask Polly to give it to us?"

"No, no," said Mark; "it's rather large. I mean to get some other things that will take up little room."

They were interrupted by a visit from Captain Walker, who came to hear how the matter had been settled with Price and Co., and where Mark was to sail to. He laughed at Mrs. Willis's fears about the fever, and said it was a famous ship the *Stratton*, and a sure captain; and as for the voyage, it was so short that she would be having the boy back before she knew, which certainly was an advantage. When next he met Mark alone, however, he shook his head, and warned him against ever sleeping a night on shore, and gave him many valuable hints about the way he ought to set to work to ingratiate himself with the captain and crew of the *Stratton*. " It's a hard life, my boy," he said; "but you can make it easier by always being ready; a willing and cheery ' Ay, ay ' goes a great way; it's only the lazy and idle who are treated harshly, as a general rule."

Mark was very busy during these days, storing his goods for barter at the bottom of his sea-chest. He did not trouble himself much about his outfit, but left that to his mother and his kind-hearted friend the organist, who proved a most valuable counsellor, and seemed to know exactly what a boy going to sea ought to have, and where it was to be bought to the saving of a good deal of money. Mark and his two little brothers were never tired of arranging and rearranging his store of small looking-glasses, strings of glass beads, and numerous odds and ends designed for barter. Much to the amusement of both Mr. Offenbach and Mrs. Willis, Harry had insisted upon sending the old horse-shoe as his share in the speculation; and Charles, not being able to coax his mamma to part with the brass kettle, had packed up an old rusty pistol, which, as it took up very little room, found a place beside the horse-shoe.

The time glided all too quickly past for poor Mrs.

Willis, but the day came at last, when, everything being ready, Mark was to go on board the barque. There is no necessity to dwell on the sad parting: suffice it to say that Mrs. Willis tried to be as composed as possible for the boy's sake, knowing that he was going out into the world to make his way that he might help her. He was rowed away at last in one of the boats belonging to the *Blue-Bell*, which Captain Walker had kindly placed at his service, and, seeing that it would be a comfort to the mother, he had jumped in beside him at the last moment to see him safely "aboard." Mr. Offenbach was with him also, which helped to break the parting for Mark; and as for Charles and little Harry, they were so anxious that he should see them waving their handkerchiefs, after they could not distinguish the figures in the boat, that they quite forgot they were not to see their brother for many, many weeks.

"Well, I hope he'll be able to get something with my pistol," said Charles. "He might get a great lump of gold; then we would go back to the old house, and keep a carriage; at any rate, I mean to buy a pony."

"And I mean to buy a pony too," said Harry; "but then we haven't got a stable to put them in. Oh, I know: I'll buy a hobby-horse, like the one the Bentlys have; we can keep *it* anywhere, you know. I do hope Mark will get a lot of money for my horse-shoe." Having this prospect to look forward to, they could scarcely understand why their mother cried so much, and fretted to have Mark back again already.

Mark was soon safely on board the *Stratton,* and as the captain was still on shore, Mr. Sprent, the second mate, received them. It turned out he was an old friend of Captain Walker's, and he readily promised to look after Mark. "We are not hard on the boys in this ship," he said, laughing in an undertone; "if they do their work well, the captain has some little pet notion about training them; but if they shirk work, there's no quarter allowed."

"Well, I don't think you will have much trouble with my young friend here," said Captain Walker, shaking the second mate by the hand before he prepared to descend the accommodation-ladder to his boat. "Good-bye, my lad," he cried; "and a good voyage to you!"

Mark watched them till they were out of sight, keeping his eyes fixed on that part of the boat where "good old Father Fritz" was sitting fluttering his handkerchief out every now and then as a last farewell greeting.

A very short time afterwards, the captain having come on board, and the tide serving, they were tugged down the river, and the steamer casting off, they lay at anchor in the King's Roads, close to a large frigate just newly arrived. It was a lovely moonlight night, and the frigate looked so grand and large in the uncertain light, that Mark felt sorry for a little to think he belonged to such a small vessel in comparison. He had been so busy all day, that he had scarcely time to think of home, and of his mother; but now that darkness had set in, and he was told he must "turn in," his heart began to feel heavy enough. His hammock was slung down in the half-deck, in a little clear space amongst the cargo, where, after tumbling out several times in his attempt to get in, he at last succeeded, and covering himself as carefully as he could, fell asleep thinking of his mother and brothers, and of the long time that must elapse before he saw them again.

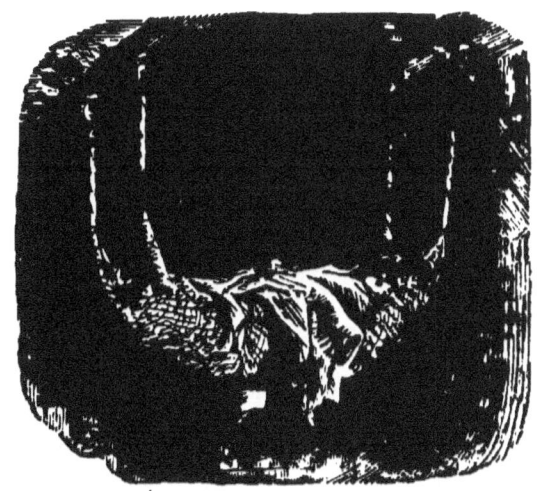

CHAPTER II.

FIRST DAYS AT SEA.

MARK was roused from a deep sleep by the sound of heavy thumps, and a wild cry, calling, " All hands to heave up anchor!" He at first doubted whether he was included in the term "hands," or not; but fearing it must be so, he hurried to get out and dress himself in haste in order to get on deck. The moon had set, and it was scarcely yet daybreak; but the tide suited, while the wind also was favourable; by help of which the *Stratton*, as soon as she had got under weigh, moved steadily away from land down the Bristol Channel.

The shipping in the roads dwindled; even the noble frigate ceased to be distinguishable from them. The surges rose longer and crisper, with wrinkling foam; the breeze freshened, till the barque, as her sails were successively hoisted, bent over from it; every now and then slowly rising erect again and balancing herself, then slanting as before, while she took long sliding plunges through the water. The spray flew, the gulls hovered, and here and there the red sail of a fishing-boat dipped up and down; on one side, from the Welsh coast, the sparkle of a lighthouse began to fade before the sunrise, which on the other side dawned splendidly over the hills of Somersetshire. Mark knew that he saw those hills for the last time for many a day, perhaps for the very last time. The waters of the Channel broadened in front, and became a flood of light, heaving and weltering awfully, like the future before him. He heard the rough pilot, with his purple face and tremendous voice, raging at every one on board, not even sparing the mates; nor would he probably have spared the captain himself, had the latter remained on deck. It was from this ill-tempered official that Mark received his first orders as one of the ship's company.

"Here, ye young useless Piawauwau," growled the pilot to the boy; "are you a passenger aboard?"

"No, sir," replied Mark, as respectfully as he thought due; "I am an apprentice."

"Thought so—one o' the hard bargains, too! Just you lay aloft then, and loose that maintawps'l; and be quick about it."

Mark hesitated for a moment, but the second mate, Mr. Sprent, in a friendly whisper, advised him to go, and showed him the way. Mark was a good climber, with a courageous spirit and a steady head, and he had often gone up the rope-ladders of vessels in dock, though never before when in motion so dizzily. He ran up now, mounted through the "lubber's-hole" in the round-top, and continued the ascent by the more difficult rigging of the top-mast; here he almost faltered, but he felt that his safety lay in hurrying on and not looking down, so he was not long in getting high enough. He knew the sail that was meant, but he did not know how to begin unfastening it, when he found he had another friend to guide him from the mast in front.

"Don't you see the end of the gasket, man?" called out a boy who was busily engaged there.

Mark loosed the sail successfully, and shouted back in reply, "Thank you!"

"Thank you for nothing," roared the boy rudely; "hail the deck, can't yer? Let 'em know all's clear—to hoist away." Mark followed his directions, but narrowly escaped being hoisted up himself with the sail, which would probably have jerked him off and sent him sheer down. He had a firm hold, however, and got safe down again to the deck—a more trying thing than the ascent had been, yet a satisfaction to have managed in that sudden way. As for the rough pilot, who shortly afterwards left the barque, outside Lundy Island, he had done Mark good by thus pushing him, as it were, straight off into the business of his profession. The brunt of the difficulty had been got over, and he did not now fear to do what a mate might order, or what a sailor might desire by way of help; besides which, the boy who had lately befriended him, though by no means of an amiable disposition, stood committed, so to speak, as a neighbourly acquaintance.

Setting things to rights and stowing them away, and

STOWING AWAY.

making certain arrangements among the cargo, was now for a number of days the main business of all. The necessary working of the ship had, of course, to be attended to; but as the weather continued steady, this did not much interfere with the other duties just mentioned.

The *Stratton* was a large barque, of about 520 tons burthen, with a crew, including the captain and mates, of twenty all told. We have said before that Mark had his hammock slung in the half-deck, which was shared with the carpenter and cooper, while the men occupied the forecastle. On the first day going out, Mark was asked by one of the apprentices who had his berth with the men, to help him carry the bread-barge along with their allowance of biscuits, which he very readily did. There he saw one or two of the men, only just recovering from the dissipation they had been indulging in on shore, lying stretched in their beds, while one or two more sat round on their chests. One very tall man, called "Long Jack," to distinguish him from Jack Jones and Jack Maurice, no sooner saw the bread-barge than he called out, "Come, silence there, all hands round;" then turning to Mark and his companion, he bade them set it in the middle, and in the most solemn manner imaginable asked a blessing on it.

Mark thought they must be a very serious set of men, especially as all had responded most heartily to Long Jack's Amen. "There, it's best to get them things attended to at oncet; that's to serve ye the whole voyage, my lads," said Long Jack; and seeing Jem, the oldest apprentice, laughing, he called out quite angrily, "What are ye grinning at there? do ye take us for heathenses? Come, I vote he be made to say one himself."

"Ay, ay!" shouted every one; and Jem was seized by two of the men and crushed down on to the deck on his knees, and made to say after Long Jack what he had repeated before. This ceremony being performed to every one's satisfaction, they set to to tidy up the place, pitching out the old pieces of rope and sails that had been stowed away there while the barque lay in the harbour.

When the selecting of the watches had taken place, Mark had been chosen by Mr. Sprent, the second mate, and he was very glad to find Jack Maurice was to be in his watch also. He had taken a fancy to him from the first, and Jack seemed inclined to treat him kindly, for once or twice he had given him a hint when he saw the boy was at a loss how to proceed. Fortunately for Mark, the weather was most favourable; and though he suffered from sea-sickness, it was only a very slight attack, and by the time they were at the mouth of the Bristol Channel he felt perfectly well, and was able to mount the rigging to take his farewell peep of England, as they stood out from the Land's End with the Lizard Point bearing on the north-east. As the ship took her departure from this point, Mr. Sprent called our hero to help him mark off the ship's course on the chart. He took such an evident interest in the operation, that the second mate offered to teach him navigation. "Do you intend to stick by the sea as a profession?" he had said kindly and with a smile; and when Mark replied in the affirmative, he said, "Well, my boy, I promised Captain Walker to look after you; but for that matter, this is the ship to come to if you really want to learn. The captain takes a sort of pride in training his apprentices, and boasts that every one passes the examinations with credit. But he'll keep you hard at it, I give you warning."

"I'm not afraid, sir," said Mark; "I am very anxious to get on as quickly as possible; and I am much obliged to you for offering to help me."

Very often through the night, during their watch, Mr. Sprent would call Mark to show him how they took an observation, or explained how the ship's course was found by the log; and sometimes the captain would do the same, seeming to take a pleasure in answering any questions Jem, the other apprentice, or Mark might ask. Captain Trehern was a man in the prime of life, stout and robust, with the repute of being able and intrepid, and, as the men said, a salt of the first water. He was rather morose and distant in his manners, but had high honourable feelings, which led him to take an interest in the boys placed under his charge; and to such an extent did he carry this notion, that his officers spoke of it as a peculiar crotchet or hobby, which, though they shrugged their shoulders at it, must be put up with. The chief mate, Mr. Yoyser, was a very intelligent man, master of his profession, but very stern and passionate, and exceedingly jealous of his authority. He was short, thick-set, and strongly built, with a weather-beaten face, a strong, muscular arm, and a fist that could have dealt a blow equal to a marlin-spike. Mr. Sprent, on the other hand, was tall, though well and firmly made, and had served a regular apprenticeship to the sea, and was an active seaman. Mr. Dodds, the third mate, called by the men "the Dickey," was a young man just newly out of his four years' apprenticeship; a hulking, clumsy young fellow, with a large face, and his feet generally in light pumps, that gave them a swelled look. As for the men, they were all pretty much alike, with the exception of Jack Maurice, who was middle-aged, and more refined in his manners. He was very much respected by both the officers and men, and though he was quiet and almost distant to his shipmates, they liked him, whispering among themselves that there was some secret trouble stowed snugly away under Jack Maurice's guernsey, that made him dullish at times. Yet occasionally he was cheery enough, and when these humours were on him he would sometimes join in spinning a yarn for the public benefit.

The *Stratton* ran swiftly on her course for many days in succession before the trade-wind from the north-east, which stood more or less south-westwards to the tropical latitudes. This sent her rolling and dipping along, for the most part with very little change of sails; sometimes with studding-sails extended on one side by booms, which made her look like a disabled bird, as she slid from one deep blue billow to another, now and then wetting the lower corners of the canvas. The flying-fish came fluttering out of the wave-sides, and occasionally fell on board, as the dolphins or the bonitoes chased them; the porpoises gambolled in a shoal across the ship's bows, and disappeared when one was struck at, though without effect, by the three-pronged "grains;" now and then a whale was seen spouting; or the great "black-finners," with horns on their backs, were seen heaving up and sinking again. The floating sea-weed soon covered the water, till the barque appeared to move through a sea of moss; and the heat, and the tossing, and the fiery glow of the brine at night, showed that they were crossing the bend of the great Gulf Stream. Sharks were seen, and the weather became more fickle, with occasional squalls, or thunder-clouds that passed as yet with a flash or two and a muttering rumble.

They spoke a ship bound homeward for England, and gave their own name, with the report "All's well;" after which the only break to the dulness as yet was the talking about the first sight they would have of land, and speculations among the few who had never crossed the Equator, how Neptune would treat them when he came on board. All this while the work of the ship had chiefly consisted of beating off rust from anchors and chain-cables, scraping the bottoms of boats, scouring brass-

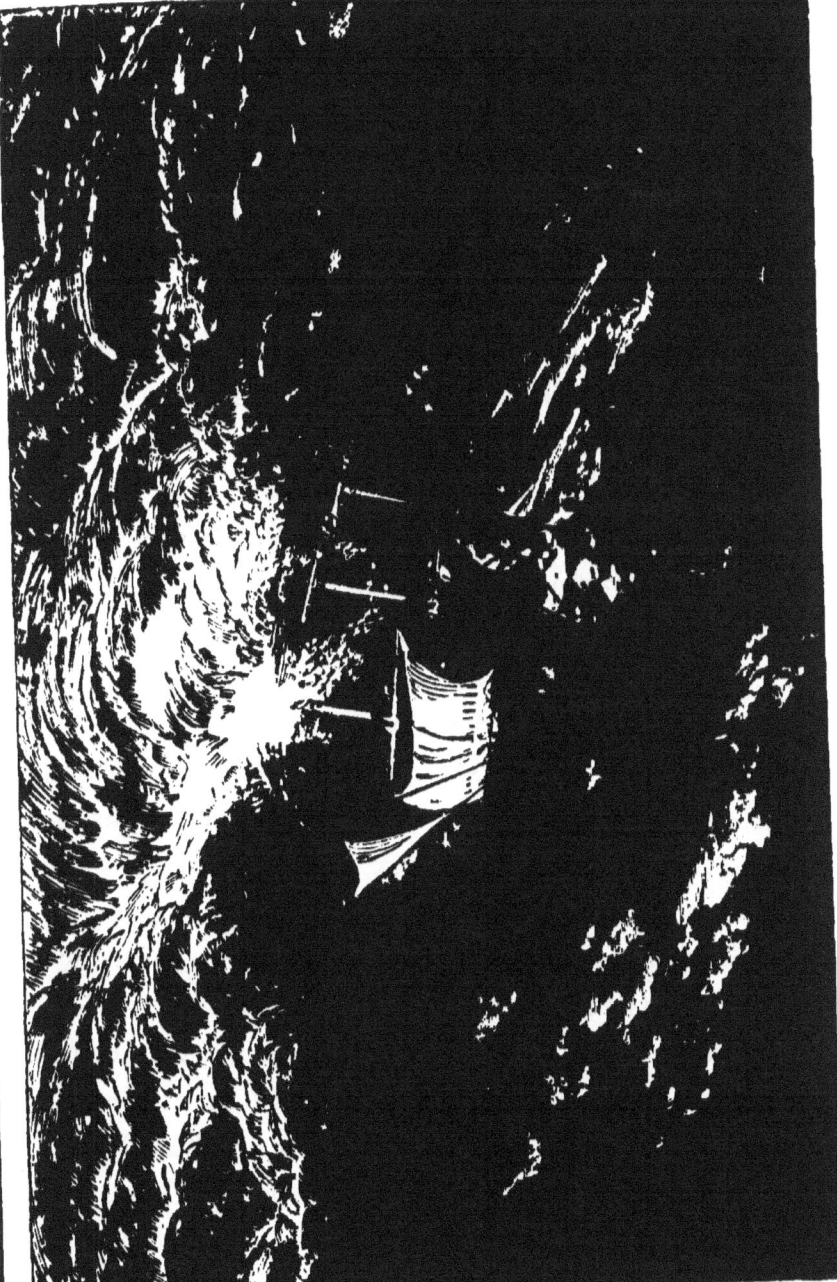

work, greasing masts, painting and mending, or making spun-yarn out of old hawsers. Very dull work, but very hard too, under the hot sun; and so important did the chief mate think it, that he kept all hands at it the whole day, not allowing the usual turn of "watches." The captain, of course, gave his authority for it all, and Mr. Yoyser quite prided himself on his own ingenuity in finding out fresh work of the kind. But a gale grew up in the midst of it, interrupting all this, much to the relief of the grumbling seamen, and certainly not less to the delight of Mark Willis. Was it for this rust-beating and pitch-scraping, thought he, that he had given up being a chorister in St. Augustin's, and hearing Mr. Offenbach's glorious music, and learning the classics, and living happily at home with his mother and little brothers, even above the despised stationer's shop? And he watched the horizon as it banked up with clouds that night before going below to his hammock, feeling scarcely afraid of the coming storm, though not a little excited.

Through his sleep he seemed to feel it growing and growing; till in the middle of a dream, that carried him peacefully back to the little parlour at Bristol, the ceiling suddenly seemed to have opened, and a great voice roared down, "All hands reef topsails! Bear a hand!"

"Ay, ay!" shouted the carpenter. "Come, tumble out, youngster," he cried; but Mark was already out and half-dressed. "Take time, my lad, and put on your jacket," he continued; "we'll have a roughish night of it, or I'm mistaken."

Mark made his way on deck as well as the violent motion of the ship would allow, but it was with the greatest difficulty he could keep his feet.

"Brace round the yards!" he heard the chief mate shouting through the trumpet; and Mark hurried forward, when the ship gave a sudden roll, and he fell flat on his face, and a heavy sea being shipped the next moment, he was nearly washed overboard; but, fortunately, Long Jack seized hold of him, and pushed him forward to a place of safety.

"Here, you young nuffing-at-all," was shouted in his ear, and Mark was pulled into the galley by black Sambo the cook. "Did you t'ink you had your sea-legs on all right? Ah, but you wrong; nebber were in a gale before. Here, drink dat," and Sambo poured out some brandy from a small flask and held it to Mark's lips.

The ship was now scudding before the wind, and the waves seemed to Mark to be running mountains high. The weather was so rough that the cook couldn't get breakfast, and with great difficulty managed to boil some coffee about noon. Everything about decks, such as boats, water-casks, and galley, had been lashed doubly fast, for the power of the wind in such a gale was tremendous. It was impossible to draw a breath when looking to windward; and, to get along decks, Mark found it was necessary to draw himself along by the bulwark or life-lines; indeed, he was often obliged to make himself fast, as the others did, to ropes stretched from the stern to the bows, so that they might be pulled along by those "aft" or "forward." There was a lull for about an hour, and Mark had been thinking it must be all over; but Jack Maurice told him it was only gathering strength, and they would have a tough night of it.

"You don't think there is great danger, do you?" said Mark, his lip quivering in spite of him when he thought of his mother.

"There's always danger, my lad," said Maurice; "but hark! there's the order for another reef; the captain sees we are to have more of it."

"Pass the word to take in another reef, Mr. Yoyser. Close-reef them this time," said the captain, who was trying to keep a footing on the quarter-deck.

The larboard or first-mate's watch had just gone below, but the one watch was considered sufficient for the present. Mark was bravely attempting to get into the mizzen-rigging to go aloft, but the captain, fearing he would tumble overboard, ordered him down, and called to him to help the mates and himself as they pulled with all their might at the rope which drew the windward end of the topsail-yard towards the storm, in order that the men might be able to pull up the sail in reefing it. The sail, however, was too much distended by the blast to let this be done, and every moment was precious.

"Luff! luff!" shouted Captain Trehern to the man at the wheel, hollowing his hand to his mouth to carry the sound. "Bring the ship to the wind, Maurice!"

The wheel did its part only too quickly in that heavy sea; for the ship flew up toward the gale, and was on the point of broaching-to, another name for destruction in the circumstances. Seeing the helmsman vainly straining to reverse the wheel again, the captain ran staggering up to his assistance.

"Call the watch, boy!" roared the captain into Mark's ear in passing. "For your life—quick!"

Mark rushed below, and roused the other men with difficulty, for they had been wearied, and had scarce fallen asleep. The immediate danger was over when they got on deck, the *Stratton* having been got sideways to the wind again; but the scene was truly a terrifying one to more experienced eyes than Mark's, and the other top-sail had still to be set right from where it hung driven into the rigging of its mast. This once done by their united efforts, the barque weathered it well; and advantage was taken of another short lull in the gale to get a low-staysail set along between her fore and main-masts, which helped to steady her from rolling. She was then, to use the nautical phrase, "brought by the wind on the starboard-tack," with her head to the northward.

Mark saw no more until he felt he was nearly up to the arm-pits in water, in which Jem was floundering, having been washed to leeward, and almost overboard. Mark caught hold of him by the hair, and then gave him a hand, which he grasped. Fortunately, all the lee-ports had been triced up, and she quickly freed herself from the immense weight of water, which otherwise must have caused her to founder. At midnight the gale was at its height; after that the sea became more regular, and consequently less dangerous; the mainstay-sail being set, the barque lay throughout the night in safety. For some days it continued to blow, without much variation as to the violence or course of the wind, during which time, as it was impossible to cook in the galley, they had to live on raw pork and biscuits. After this the wind moderated, and the sea went down. All necessary sail was set, and once more they stood on their course. A very few days after land was sighted from the mast-head, which proved to be the lofty Peak of Teneriffe, which showed itself high above the clouds, more than a hundred miles distant. Early the next morning they anchored at Santa Cruz, capital of the island of Teneriffe, when, to the captain's great indignation and dismay, he was informed by the health-officer they must ride out a quarantine of eight days. After breakfast Mr. Sprent went in one of the boats to the mole with some orders from the captain, and, to Mark's great delight, he was allowed to accom-

PEAK OF TENERIFFE.

pany him, though they were not permitted to land. Jack Maurice was also one of the boat's crew, and while they waited in the boat, he held an animated conversation in Spanish with some of the men who stared at them from the shore. They were the most wretched-looking objects that Mark had ever seen. Some were dressed in coarse shirts and trousers, while others of them had no shirts at all; and many of the boys had a covering of some kind, made of goat's-skin.

"I wish we could go on shore and see the island," said Mark to Jack Maurice. "Do you think it is likely we shall be allowed to do it before we sail?"

"Well, I don't think so, my boy," replied Maurice. "I hear we're to go to another of these islands, either Grand Canary or Gomero, and there won't be a minute of spare time."

"How I should like to climb to the top of that mountain," said Mark. "I wonder if any person has ever managed to reach the very pinnacle?"

"Oh yes," said Maurice, laughing. "Why, for that matter, I've been up myself; and a tough business it was, I can tell you."

"You, Maurice!" said Mark, in some surprise. "Oh, I wish you would tell me about it."

"Not now, my boy," said Maurice kindly; "for here comes the order to out oars and pull aboard; but when we have a spell of leisure time, mayhap I'll give you the whole yarn of that expedition ashore."

Mark often thought that if Maurice's history was known it would be worth hearing; he was such a superior man to any of the others, and knew so much about different countries, and their manners and customs, that Mark was often surprised. He generally took care, however, not to show his knowledge before his shipmates, always saying in a whisper, with a quiet laugh, "It's not a comfortable thing, my lad, to be set down as a sea-lawyer; in the fo'ks'l they'd call it book-talk, if they heard it, so we'll keep it quiet between ourselves." Yet he always seemed glad to have a quiet hour with Mark, and would answer any amount of questions the boy chose to ask. The very first opportunity Mark claimed Maurice's promise, and mounting the rigging, they got into the round-top, their favourite place of retreat. Maurice stood for some time with his eyes fixed on the land, and his arms crossed, and with a strange abstracted look in his face, that always made Mark wish and long to hear more about his history. But it was impossible to draw anything from him of a personal character; for Mark had heard some of the men saying he did not like to be questioned, and had even turned away from his questioner with an angry oath—the only time he had ever been heard to make use of a wrong word.

"Ay, my boy," he said, with a sigh, "the last time I was in this harbour it was under very different circumstances. Hark ye, if I tell ye some of my past life, not a word of it below. Yes; when I lay here last, I was boatswain of a large foreign craft; but that's neither here nor there. Here I am nothing but an A B aboard this barque *Stratton;* and what's more, I'm likely to keep that to the end of the chapter, as the saying is. Well, when I was a youngster like you I was crazy about seeing the world. I used to read dozens of books of travel and adventure; from that I determined to see the places myself, so there wasn't a port I touched at, no matter where, but I managed to get ashore and see everything there was to be seen. When I was aboard the Spaniard that I mentioned, we touched at this port, and by the captain's orders I set out with a gentleman passenger we had aboard to climb that mountain. I remember reading somewhere that Teneriffe means the White Mountain, the peak being mostly always covered with snow. It was about four o'clock one afternoon we set out on horseback to visit the Peak. We had a muleteer with us, and a guide. After ascending about six miles, we arrived towards sunset at the most distant habitation from the sea, which was in a hollow, and here we found an aqueduct of open troughs or spouts, that conveyed the water down from the head of the hollow. Here our servants watered the horses, and filled some small barrels with water to serve us on our expedition. While this was being done my companion and I walked into the hollow, which was very pleasant, being full of trees that gave out a strong sweet smell. Near the houses were some fields of maize and Indian corn; and we were told that on several parts on this side of the island they had two crops of it in the year.—But we might be more comfortable, Mark, my boy," he interrupted himself to say, " if we took a seat on the foretopsail-yard there," pointing above; and when they were comfortably seated, and Maurice had lighted his pipe, he proceeded,—

"Mounting again, we travelled for some time on a steep road, and got into the woods and the clouds just as it grew dark, but fortunately, owing to the road being bounded with laurel and brushwood, we could not lose our way. We went on for about a mile further, till we came to the upper edge of the wood above the clouds, where we alighted, made a fire, and had our supper, and went to sleep under the bushes. A little after ten, the moon shining brightly, we mounted again, and travelled for two hours over a very bad road; but this brought us to a part covered with shingle, which we rode over for about an hour at a pretty good pace. The air now began to be sharp and cold, and the wind blew strong from the south-west. By the advice of our guide we alighted here, intending to rest till about four in the morning, as there was a cave where we might sleep; the mouth of it was built up to about a man's height to prevent the wind and cold from getting in, and we lighted a great fire with some dry shrubs we found scattered about, and fell asleep; but we soon wakened again, for our skin itched so dreadfully that we fancied it must be caused by a plague of fleas, but our guide explained it was owing to the cold thin air, want of rest, and sleeping in our clothes. We crept very close to the fire, so close that one side was nearly scorched while the other was benumbed with cold, so that we spent a most miserable night.

"In the morning we set out again; but the road being so steep, we were compelled to leave the horses in the charge of one of the servants, and go the rest of the way on foot. We walked hard to keep ourselves warm, and after much fatigue, owing to the steepness of the road, and the loose and sandy soil, we reached the top of a rising hill. Here we found a great many huge loose stones, some of them about ten feet every way, and though the road was not so steep, we were compelled to leap from one to another of these stones. Among them we found a cavern, and in it a well. Some poor people, who earn a living by gathering brimstone, put down a ladder, and we went down by it into the cavern. We found it was spacious within, almost ten yards wide and twenty in height, and covered with water except just where the feet of the ladder stood. The water, two fathoms deep, was there frozen to the inner edges of the cave; and when we tried to drink of it we couldn't, it was so dreadfully cold. Another quarter or half a mile brought us to the bottom of the real peak, or sugar-loaf, which is very steep. Though it is only about half a mile in length, it was so difficult to climb—owing to the intense cold and the loose, crumbling side—we were forced to stop, I believe, forty times to rest ourselves, as our hearts panted and beat fearfully. When we set out

in the morning, the sun was just coming out of the clouds, which were spread out under us at a great distance downward. We saw from the peak the tops of several of the other islands, and they seemed to be strangely near us. When we were rested we began to look about us. We found the peak is hollow, like a bell, and the bottom of this caldron is about forty yards wide; and in many places we saw smoke and steam coming out in puffs. The heat of the ground was very great, and we even felt it through the soles of our shoes. The brimstone here seemed to be of all colours, azure, blue, green, violet, yellow, and scarlet. All the top of the island shows evident marks of some terrible convulsion that has happened in Teneriffe; for the sugar-loaf is nothing else than earth mixed with ashes and stones, thrown out of the bowels of the earth, and the great square stones I spoke of before, when the peak was a volcano.

"We had got up all safe enough, and now, after seeing everything of any consequence, and admiring the extraordinary and uncommon appearance of the clouds below us at a great distance, we began to think of going down again, when—"

" Oh, do tell me how the clouds looked!" said Mark, interrupting Jack.

" Well, they seemed like the ocean, only the surface of them was not so blue or smooth; but they had the appearance of very white wool; and where this cloudy ocean, as we may call it, touched the shore, it seemed to foam like billows breaking on it. We then turned to go down, but Mr. Tibbit, our passenger, made us stop till he had rolled over a large piece of rock for some scientific purpose of his own. He was a short man—or rather, his legs were far too short for his body, which was built on a large enough scale—and in giving the final push he lost his balance, and away went the stone, with him rolling after it, down the steep side. Fortunately he had not rolled down the steepest side, else he would never have been seen more—for we had already pitched some stones over from that quarter, and they rolled quite out of sight—but it was quite steep enough, I can tell you; and there I had to dig my way down, making steps in the side of the hill as well as I could, with the help of the guide, till we reached the unfortunate gentleman. Another stone had rolled over of itself after he slipped, and had pinned him firmly by the skirts of his coat, and the danger was, if he moved, the stone would push him still further down. There he sat, yelling and crying out that he was slipping, and offering large sums of money to us if we saved him. We got him hauled up at last by the help of the guide's stick and our belts; but I got my left hand severely cut, as you may see by the mark it has left, caused by another rock rolling down and crushing it before I was aware it was upon me. So, you see, I bear the stamp of Teneriffe on me still."

"Starboard watch, ahoy!" now sounded from below, and both of them had to hurry down. Mark was still more puzzled about Jack Maurice, and unable to make out how, once being a boatswain, he had not risen higher, instead of being reduced to sail as a common seaman; for as he went on he spoke in a way that showed he had been something better in former days, and had received a very fair education.

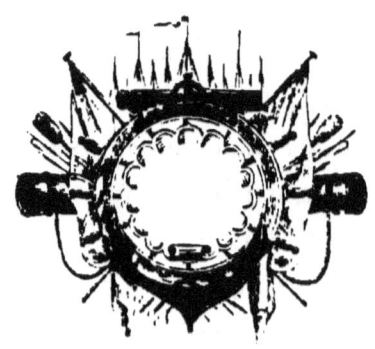

CHAPTER III.

DOWN THE TROPICS.

FOR a few days there was enough of occupation to keep them from wearying in preparing a part of the hold to take on board the wine destined as a portion of her cargo for home, as it was known it improved by being taken to a hot climate.

Besides this, Mr. Yoyser set every spare hand to repair the rigging, so that Mark had scarcely a moment's leisure. But a day before the quarantine expired, Maurice called to him to lend a hand at the sail he was mending, and Mark gladly seated himself to the task.

"I am glad our quarantine is nearly at an end now," said Mark. "I'm very anxious to get to Africa; for somehow I think it will be a much more interesting place than here. I've read a good deal about the strange trees in Africa, for one thing; and then the natives are so savage; but here it's all so tame."

"There's a lot of interesting things to be seen here

though, for all that," said Maurice. " I'll be bound you would like to see the caves they turn into houses in some parts of these islands; and as for trees, there isn't a stranger one to be seen anywhere than the raining-tree of the Canaries."

"The raining-tree! why, what is it like?" said Mark.

"It is a kind of laurel, and has very wide-spreading branches. Every morning a mist comes up from the sea and rests on the thick leaves, and then oozes out by drops during the day. The trees spring from the rocks at the end of some of the long narrow valleys, and this helps to attract the mist all the better. It is an evergreen, and grows to a great size. The water that drops from it supplies every family in the neighbourhood, and there are regular people appointed to give out the supplies."

"It must be the most curious tree that ever grew," said Mark; "don't you think so, Maurice, or do you know of any others?"

"Well, I have seen one more curious still," replied Maurice; "that was the cow-tree; and I have been told of one like the raining-tree here, called the pitcher-plant, but I've never seen it myself. I've heard this tree has a sort of small bag, shaped like a pitcher, at the foot of the stalk of each leaf, with a neatly-fitted lid, and having a kind of hinge that passes over the handle of the pitcher and joins it to the leaf. The pitcher-plant is often covered with birds, all sipping the water out of the lids they open to catch the rain; but no sooner has the cloud passed away than the goblet closes itself firmly, so that the plant always keeps some for its own nourishment."

"And the cow-tree," said Mark, "what is it like?"

"It grows in South America, in one of the most unfruitful parts of it. It clings to the steep side of a rock, and has dry, corky-like leaves, and its large woody roots can hardly find sufficient depth of soil to grow in. For several months no rain falls upon it, but the pores are so constructed as to suck in the heavy dews that fall every night in hot countries. But though the leaves look dry and the branches seem to be dead, when the trunk is pierced out comes a sweet kind of milk. You get the most of it just at sunrise, and the natives there crowd from all quarters to fill their bowls for their breakfasts."

"Well, it's all very curious," said Mark. "I have heard of a butter-tree, and I believe it grows in Africa, but I never heard of a cow-tree before. There must be every kind of thing, in plants and trees, that one needs."

"Ay, my boy," said Maurice, "this is a wonderful world; and people lose a good deal of pleasure, I can tell you, by going about it with their eyes shut. I've been with many a shipmate ashore at some strange port, and they would laugh at me for wanting to go into the country to see what sort of trees, and birds, and animals were to be found. They liked much better to get drunk at some drinking-shed; for there's always rum to be had, somehow, at the smallest port that is, if there's nothing else."

"Well, Maurice, I only hope we shall be allowed to get ashore together at the Gaboon, that's all," said Mark, laughing. "I promise you I'll keep my eyes very wide open indeed." This being a good opportunity, Mark confided to his companion the notion he had of trading in a small way on his own account, which seemed to amuse the worthy seaman not a little, but he heartily entered into the idea, and promised to lend a helping hand.

The casks of wine were not long of being secured in the hold, along with some hogsheads of barilla, and the *Stratton* proceeded again without delay on her course. The only circumstance of any consequence that happened between their leaving the port of Santa-Cruz and the Gaboon River was an encounter with a waterspout. The weather had been very sultry and hot, and clouds began to gather heavily, and a sudden squall came on. The sea appeared to be raised in a great heap, and whirled and bubbled, the upper part being lost in the mass of spray and foam, which was driven rapidly round. The column moved slowly forward, sometimes quite straight, sometimes being curved, and again taking a twisted form. On it came with a rushing noise, like the roar of a cataract, making the barque quiver from stem to stern. Fortunately, the second mate had observed it in time, and had

WATERSPOUT.

ordered the foremost carronade to be got ready, when it was discharged at it with such good effect that it gradually became more transparent, and vanished into the clouds. Every one heaved a sigh of relief as it thus disappeared, for, but for Mr. Sprent's promptitude, the vessel might have been dismasted, and left a total wreck. That evening, in the second dog-watch, or between the hours of six and eight, many stories were related about these strange phenomena of Nature. After several yarns had been spun by the older hands, Peter, the cabin-boy, who was listening very earnestly, suddenly said, "Oh, but I could tell you about a stranger spout than any o' yourn," and he turned up his small nose with a strong expression of contempt.

"Ay, boy, could ye?" said Long Jack; "then out with it; but mind ye, if ye don't make your words good, I'll try the weight o' this rope-end across ye—it'll help to take some o' your impudence and fool-hardiness out o' ye, mayhap."

"Come, now, don't frighten the youngster," said Jack Jones, instituting himself as umpire. "Let's have the yarn, boy, and we'll see you get fair play."

Peter, who was by no means easily put down, as Mark knew to his cost, gave a hitch to his belt, and began his story in the most approved seaman's style. "It was in the Indian Ocean that the ship I sailed my first voyage in lay becalmed. She was a big lump of a brig, and sailed as if she was water-logged. Well, there we were, in as dead a calm as ever ye see'd, when all of a sudden the waters got black as ink, and the sea rose in mountains over the ship's side, and away we went almost flying through the water. Every one of us was shinning up the rigging like mad to stow the sails, and I had just got out on a yard to pass round the weather gasket, when down comes a great black cloud, and up goes the sea to meet it close to our bows, and the two together lifts our lump of a brig up, and away it goes with us flying through the air. We hadn't time to give ourselves up for lost when down it dropped us with such a crash that the mainmast jumped right out of its socket; and if it hadn't been for the ropes and tackle, would have shot itself right up into the clouds, like the arrow from a bow. But that wasn't the strangest part of it, for on taking our bearings, what does the captain find but we had been carried as much as a good three days' sail, and instead o' being near to the Chagos Islands, we had been blown back to the Cape of Good Hope, a distance of—"

"Hold hard, ye young rascal!" cried Long Jack. "None o' your crammers. We're not to be took in wi' sich stuff."

"I tell ye it's true. Was I not there myself? And what's more, if ye ax any man ye meet at the Cape, he'll say the same. For there was a laugh against the captain, d'ye see? For when the waterspout caught up the brig, it took the captain, who was walking about the quarter-deck, and whirled him up like a feather; and there's no saying but what he may have been took up into the blue sky altogether, and set astride a star or some'at, had he not caught hold of the truck, and then slid down the skysail-mast to the rigging. He told us about it next day, and we grinned at it. But, d'ye see, he wore a wig; and, sure enough, his head was as bare as my hand, and his wig was nowhere to be found. The next morning, when I was aloft, I see'd something fluttering out from the truck; and I climbed up to see what it could be—for it looked like some strange bird—when what was this but the captain's best wig a-hanging like a red pennant; and, moreover—"

"Hold hard!" shouted some of the men, though they could not keep from laughing either. "Give him a taste of the rope's-end, Jack, to teach him to spin sich yarns to his betters."

But Peter had already made off, and had escaped to a place of safety, grinning from ear to ear.

A day or two after this, Mark was up the rigging, when he observed a strange bird seated on the fore-topgallant yard. The weather was rough at the time, and the sail was close furled, the vessel leaning over a good deal; but in spite of this he made his way cautiously out along the foot-rope to have a better view of it, when to his surprise it sat quite still, and allowed him to come close up to it. He then stretched out his hand, but to his further surprise it allowed him to catch hold of it, merely uttering a rough hoarse cry. Mark was not long in carrying his prize down below, when the captain, who happened to be on the deck, observed him.

MARK CATCHING A BOOBY.

"Oh, so you've managed to catch a booby, have you?" he said, taking it out of Mark's hands.

"Is it a booby, sir?" said Mark. "I have read about them; but I thought it was a dark bird, only having gray and brownish colours about it, and black feet and bill. Now this one has a brown back, white breast, and pink bill."

"Yes; but this is a booby, my boy. The one you have read about is a noddy: indeed, I believe they all belong to the same family; though, more properly speaking, the booby belongs to the Gannet or Solan Goose family. But what are you going to do with this specimen?"

"Well, I don't know, sir," said Mark. "I should like to keep it very much; but, I suppose, I could not manage it."

"You might get the steward to show you how to stuff it," said the captain.

But Mark did not like the idea of taking the bird's life after allowing itself to be caught in such a quiet manner. "I think if I cannot keep it alive, sir," he said, "I will give it its liberty."

"Well, then, look at this," said the captain, who had been watching something in the water.

And Mark stepped forward, and looking to where the captain pointed, saw a fish floating on the top of a wave, evidently in a death struggle.

"He has received some deadly wound from an adversary below," said the captain. "Now fling the booby up in the air."

Mark did as the captain told him; and the next

moment the bird had swooped down on the dying fish, and appeared to swallow it up bodily, though it seemed to be larger than itself. A few moments after, something dark came fluttering down, as if from the clouds themselves, but the ship was passing too rapidly on her course for Mark to make out distinctly what it was.

"Ah," said the captain, "see how everything falls a prey to one another! There has been a frigate-bird overhead, and he has swooped down to force the booby to disgorge the fish he has swallowed, for the 'frigate' is the great enemy of the stupid *Sula fusca*, or booby. On the islands and rocky shores where the booby settles, they catch fish all day long for the benefit of those voracious birds who are waiting to attack and rob them; for the frigate-birds can neither swim nor dive, and the only fish they can take for themselves is the flying-fish. But they are the swiftest birds that range the ocean."

Mark was quite sorry when the captain turned to go to the cabin, for he spoke so kindly that it was impossible not to feel interested in the conversation. But he had to be content; for though he would have liked to have asked some questions about the other sea-birds, he knew it was a great condescension and a stretch of good-nature and courtesy for the commander of the good barque *Stratton* to take any notice whatever of a mere ship's apprentice.

The wind being favourable, they reached the mouth of

the Gaboon River late in the evening, and anchored five miles from land. It was impossible for Mark to sleep that night; and it felt so stifling below, that he flung himself down at one of the open ports to wait impatiently for morning. Hitherto his life at sea had been monotonous enough, and the work by no means agreeable, but that was now a thing of the past, when he realized that he was close to the land. With all his old ideas of the delight of first beholding a strange great country like Africa, he kept peering into the gloom towards the shore, in the vain endeavour to make out the form of the woods, the slopes, the mountains, with the opening of the wide river, and the uncouth huts and fantastic structures he expected to see. At any rate, he enjoyed what is the most thrilling pleasure of this kind ever experienced by the novice at sea—the blended hum of the multitudinous noises of the forest, occasionally breaking out into separate notes, with now and then the still more exciting sounds produced by human inhabitants, whilst the very smell of the earth and leaves came wafted by the fitful land-breeze to the deck. Always uppermost in his mind, however, came his fancy about bartering with the natives, by means of his small stock of articles prepared for the purpose, in order to obtain possession of gold dust, ivory, and such valuables, which the African coast produced. He had his mother's benefit in view; a consideration rising in his mind, through warm affection, above even the boyish delight in adventure and in seeing the world for its own sake.

When day broke next morning, he was considerably

SCENE ON THE WEST COAST OF AFRICA.

disappointed at the general appearance of the land. It was low, on the whole, though overspread with wild wood; here and there topped by feathery palms, and parted by lines of plumy cocoa-nut trees along the shore. A streak of white sand ran beneath them, on either side of the wide opening of the river, which sent its dingy flood to mingle gradually with the green of the sea, which expanded away in all the exquisite blueness of the tropical ocean. On one side of the entrance to the Gaboon was the inner anchorage, with the trade settlement and native village beyond, backed by a slight eminence, on which the factory stood, with a flag waving over it, and some appearance of rude fortification. Two or three merchant vessels, with their decks roofed over, lay before it; and, to Mark's great delight, further out was a man-of-war steam cruiser, showing British flags. Still further out, a great canoe full of people, both native and European, appeared to be on its way to the cruiser; in the middle of it was raised something like an immense umbrella, and an awning besides; while at the same time an English ensign was displayed from a flagstaff above. As it approached the cruiser, a salute was fired from the latter, showing that some important personage must be at hand. It was, indeed, no other than the chief African potentate of the river—His Majesty King Glass himself. Here was something already answering to our hero's expectations, and it was not long before he was favoured by an opportunity of seeing things more closely at the Gaboon.

The *Stratton* still lay outside the bar, over which there was not always sufficient water to take vessels safely at that season, till the tides reached a greater height. Such being the case, the jolly-boat was ordered to be lowered away, as the captain was going to send his "list" of articles for sale to a resident merchant for inspection; and also to make arrangements to pay the king's "dash," or harbour dues. Mr. Sprent was to go, with five of the best hands on board, as the boat might be difficult to manage in crossing the bar.

Mark ventured to say in a whisper to the second mate, "May I go too, sir?"

And looking down at the boy's anxious face, he replied, "Well, perhaps you may. But it's a rough passage, and not free from danger."

"Oh, I don't mind that a bit, sir," said Mark, hastily, but with due respect, making Mr. Sprent laugh outright at his eagerness. And accordingly, when the boat was ready, Mark was the first to step into her.

They now approached the bar, or that under-water bank of sand and mud across the entrance of the river, which is always found towards the mouths of the great African streams, and of which there are sometimes two or three even in succession. Although the *Stratton*, with her cargo, could not safely get across this, there was at present in such still water no sign of the obstruction, except here and there a wandering streak, or a winding patch of the brown river-water, almost distinct from the green and blue of the sea. Another mark of its presence, in a more alarming way, was suddenly visible in the shape of two or three back-fins of ground-sharks, which rose black and wet over the surface where the boat crossed, seeming to follow it with an interest that made the boy shiver. The slight danger soon passed, however, after which these odious objects vanished; and it was not long before the boat fairly entered the river and steered to the landing-place. They had not reached this, indeed, before an additional illustration of the dangers to be found in an African river became visible to Mark. On the hot mud under the opposite bank—near a low thicket of the tangled mangroves, whose roots were left bare by the tide—there lay what Mark took for three or four drifted logs, or fallen stems of trees, with the bark half off. One of the men, as he pulled his oar, gave a meaning sign to Mark.

"What do you think these are, lad?" he whispered, looking over his shoulder.

Mark followed his glance, and saw a slight motion of one of the supposed logs. It seemed to roll itself up a little more, stretching itself full in the sun, till he made out the shape of a hideous foot, and saw, with a start, a pair of huge jaws yawning drowsily, as it were, in the distance.

"A crocodile!" he exclaimed, in the same undertone.
"Yes; it must be."

"Alligators," muttered the seaman, scowling, as if he had some unpleasant recollection in connection with them. "Sink the brutes!—I wish I had but a slap at 'em!"

On shore, a sort of procession was in movement in the direction of the harbour, which proved to be "Will Glass," the king's nephew, on his way to pay a visit to the steam cruiser. He was followed by six or seven of his numerous wives, and was arrayed in a full-dress English uniform, said to have cost upwards of £60.

During this time, Mr. Sprent was busily engaged with one of the resident merchants, making arrangements for the exchange of the *Stratton's* cargo of " assorted notions " for the produce of the country, which in this case was to be palm oil, gold dust, and ivory.

The list having been put up conspicuously in the merchant's store, so that the traders, purchasers, and idlers might see what was for sale, and all the other arrangements being made, he returned to the boat, where the men and Mark soon joined him. It was late in the afternoon when the boat left the landing-place, on its way back to the ship. The sky had darkened, and a squall of some kind was evidently about to come off the land; if, indeed, something more violent was not to be feared. This quickened the movements of the boat's crew; and they pushed briskly off, bending to the oars with a will. On reaching the mouth of the river, however, they found the water beginning to bubble like a boiling caldron, through which they could make but slow way. Before them there was now real danger on the bar, increased by the state of the weather. When they had first entered, the time of high-water was not far past, but it was now the extreme ebb, or low-water, so that the bar became terribly distinct. It formed one broad band

CROSSING THE BAR.

of roaring surf, shaped like a half-moon, round the mouth of the river, without a break that could be discovered to escape through. Happily for them, there was an advantage for the moment from the very approach of the squall, if rightly taken in time, but which insured their destruction if they delayed.

"Step the mast there!" cried Mr. Sprent, as the first puffs of heavy air began to blow from over the woods. "Up with the sail—quick, for your lives, men!"

It was done; and the ropes that drew down the lower corners of the canvas were hauled to their place, Mark being stationed by the mate at the more important of the two, while Mr. Sprent himself watched for the right moment to steer between the angry surges as they ran together into foam.

"Now, boy," said he hoarsely, "our lives depend on you letting go when I give the word; but I will trust you."

Mark answered by a glance of grateful determination, and away the boat went, oars and sail jointly shooting the boat far in and up on the rising breaker. They outran it, and were tossed on, heaving sideways up to another.

"Pull all—bend and break 'em!" shouted the mate. "Now in-oars—hold on with the sheet, my boy." There was a moment when they seemed flung helplessly away, and all that Mark could do was to cling to his seat, with the precious rope clutched in his hands. He thought of the sand-bank below, and of the horrible ground-sharks that came to mind with it. One skilful turn of the rudder by Mr. Sprent, and they were safe so far; but the squall was upon them next moment, with a whistle and a howl, sending the spray along into their eyes.

"Let go the sheet!" cried the mate, and it flew loose at the word. "Down sail—out oars!" The free waves of the open water were beneath them, and on went the boat, the rowers pulling stoutly for the ship, which they soon reached in safety.

By that time a regular tornado was upon them; one startling flash of lightning after another, with terrific peals of thunder between, told what would have been the boat's fate if it had been delayed a little longer. The wind roared through the rigging, the rain fell by bucketfuls in one continuous stream, and the vessel groaned at her anchor, rolling from side to side. Still the cable held well, and she rode it out unhurt. By midnight the worst was past, and the weather turned by degrees to its former course.

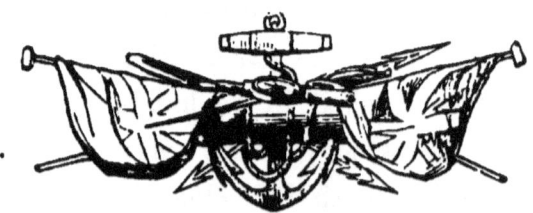

CHAPTER IV.

AFRICAN COAST-TRADE.

NEXT day, with the help of the flood-stream from inland, the tide enabled them to be piloted up to the proper moorings inside, when the *Stratton* was then housed over in the customary way with awnings and deals; after which she proceeded with the regular trade of the place. The necessary kroomen were on board, who were to attend to the boat service; and the captain had departed for his residence on shore, leaving the vessel in the charge of the mates, who, with the crew, were to despatch and receive the cargo. For a time every one was so much occupied, that Mark had no opportunity of attending to his own speculations, and had half given up the idea of it altogether, when one day Peter, the cabin-boy, tapped him on the shoulder, and beckoning to him in a mysterious way, disappeared up the rigging, where our hero was not long in following him. When he had reached the

round-top, he found Peter standing with a small basket in his hand, evidently having some very precious articles there, judging by the careful way in which he was holding it. Mark had been somewhat surprised at Peter's summons, for they had never been very good friends all the voyage; Peter delighting to teaze and worry Mark on any and every occasion. To such a height had he carried his mischievous tricks, that only two days before they had reached the Gaboon, Mark had determined to free himself in a most effective manner from his tormentor, and, accordingly, he had turned upon Peter, and after a severe fight, the men being there to see everything was "fair and above board," Mark was declared the victor. They both bore the marks of the conflict on their faces, and Peter had only been able to have the bandage taken off his eye that very morning. Mark was therefore more than surprised to hear that Peter wanted to ask his advice in a friendly way, and to discover that this boy also, like himself, had notions of trading with the natives; nay, what was more to the point, he seemed to know how to set about it.

"I say, shipmate," he said, as Mark's head appeared above the edge of the round-top, "if you like I'll put you up to a thing or two at this here coast. But what am I saying? It isn't likely such a greenhorn as you be's, has thought of bringing aught to barter with the natives."

"There you are mistaken," said Mark; "I'm not quite so green as you think, for I've got a lot of things. I brought them on purpose."

"Well, now, who'd have a-thought he'd have known it!" said Peter, surveying him out of his right eye and screwing up his left, in imitation of Jack Jones.

"But what have you brought me up here for?" said Mark. "Was it to look at that basket of yours? have you got your private cargo stowed in there?"

"You're about right there," said Peter, beginning to unfasten the lid; "and what's more, I mean to give you a private peep;" then drawing himself up, he began to call out as he had heard some showmen do in Bristol: "Gather round, tumble round, gather round; the show is about to commence. Here you will see as rare a show of African fetiches as ever your eyes see'd. They are destined to become the property of his African majesty, King Piawauwau, and his threescore of wives; likewise there's here a valibble assortment of leg-rings, wrist-rings, and nose-rings,—all for these same queens and princesses, and lovely dears they will look with them—"

"Come, Peter, stop your nonsense," said Mark, beginning to lose patience, and sitting down on the floor, preparatory to going off altogether; "if you mean to show me the things, do it at once,—the watch will be called directly."

PETER SHOWING HIS TREASURES.

"Well, then, shut your eyes and open your mouth—no, I mean *wisy wersa*, as the captain said this morning."

Mark opened the lid of the basket, and to his surprise the principal objects that were packed away were two small dolls, very nicely dressed. "Why, whatever can have possessed you to bring out dolls to Africa?" said Mark, laughing heartily.

"I knowed he was green," said Peter, taking out the dolls very cautiously, and showing the further contents of his basket. "You wait a few days, and see if my dolls won't bring in more than all your cargo put together. Now, what do you think of these, then, by way of a change?"

"I should suppose they will be as valuable as the dolls," said Mark. "I do declare, they are some old window-curtain rings!"

"Right again, my boy," said the incorrigible Peter; "I bought the whole boiling o' them at a broker's shop for half-a-crown; and here's the small uns that hooked into the big uns."

"But what will you do with them?" said Mark.

"Sell them to the king, in course; doesn't his wives wear dozens of sich on their legs and arms! The little uns, they're for the noses; or if they don't like them for that, why then I takes this wire,—I twist off a piece so, I ties it on so, and says I, 'Ladies fair—I begs your parding—ladies black, here's ear-rings for you in a trice.'"

This seemed to be the whole contents of the basket,

with the exception of a small bag of cowrie-shells, a few red glass beads, and two old pocket-knives.

"What made you think of the rings?" said Mark, beginning to think Peter was not to be despised; "were you ever here before?"

"No; and don't mean to come again, if I knows it," replied Peter; "but I'll tell you how I happens to get them: our ship lay for some weeks 'longside of a brig that had just come in from Africa, and one o' the boys and I got very thick, and he told me a lot about the place, and what a deal he could have made if he had only taken out some things; so, when I comes to hear we were bound for this port, I goes on shore and smuggles them things aboard, and stows them away snug. I'll tell you what it is, shipmate, you may thank your stars you are aboard this ship, for in many a one the men would search your chest, and walk off with everything valibble they took a fancy to; but they knows better aboard the *Stratton* than to touch the boys' things."

"Was it your friend that told you about the dolls?" said Mark, laughing.

"Yes, it was; it was his own idea, certainly, and see if it doesn't turn out a good one. He was about the longest headed chap I ever see'd; 'cos why, he was a Yankee born, and they know what they are about, let me tell you."

"But how are you going to manage to barter your things?" inquired Mark.

"That's the rub," said Peter. "Now, in course, I have been turning the matter over, as you may be sure. I have been keeping my ears pretty wide open, for I hears a good deal of the talk going on in the cabin. This is the skipper's second trip to this quarter, and he knows the ways of the place. He lost a good deal of his cargo last time, by trusting it to some o' them native carriers."

"How was that?" said Mark; "did they steal it?"

"Well, some folks would call it stealing. You see, these men get the cargo, and take it away up into the country to sell, promising to bring back goods in exchange. Well, they often take such a time about it, a-purpose to tire out the captains, that the ships are forced to leave before they come back, if they ever do come back."

"And what is the captain going to do now?" said Mark. "The merchants here seem to be pretty well supplied."

"Yes, another day or two will finish the market here," said Peter; "and so the captain is thinking of sending the native gold-taker and a boat's crew up one of the rivers, to a place where he fancies trade can be carried on with the natives themselves, after which there's a talk that we are to sail for some other part of the coast."

"But what has all this to do with us and our chance of bartering the things we have?" said Mark.

"Just this," replied Peter: "Jack Maurice was in last

night speaking to the mates, for Jack knows this coast, and can speak a little Spanish or some other foreign lingo. He's going in the boat, and so is Mr. Sprent. Now, I was a-thinking, if you get Maurice to speak a word for us, we might be took too. I know you are a sort of a chum of Jack's; but if you got me took with you, I'd help you to get along, for I know they'll cheat you, they are so cunning, and you *are* so green."

Mark passed over the last remarks; but willingly promised to do his best to get them both included in the boat's crew. That same afternoon the captain came on deck, and after he had gone ashore again, Peter managed to give Mark, who was standing beside the chief mate, a nudge, and a knowing wink and a shrug. By this Mark understood there was some important piece of information to be communicated. When the mate had gone away, Mark proceeded up into the round-top, where he was not disappointed in finding Peter. It seemed that the captain had intimated that no more cargo was to be sent ashore; but as he was very anxious to push on, a boat was to be got in readiness to start early next morning.

"You see, the captain he says we have just arrived in the nick of time, seeing that it was a day or two after the beginning of 'the little dry season,' as them darkies call it. It only lasts six weeks, and down comes the rain for months after."

"Well, then, we had better make good use of our time now," said Mark, laughing. "I'll go and look for Maurice directly."

After a little persuasion Maurice was prevailed upon to get them both taken, and Mark made up a parcel of his goods, including the horse-shoe and pocket-pistol. He also had a small pocket-compass, and an old pinchbeck watch, the sight of which nearly drove Peter crazy with delight. These things were carefully hidden about their bodies, by the ingenious Peter, who explained that only one thing was to be shown at once.

To the boys' intense satisfaction, they were permitted to go; and though the boat was to leave at a very early hour, they were ready long before the hour of starting.

"What have you done with your dolls?" said Mark. "Have you got them with you?"

"In course; it's not very likely I'd have left them behind," said Peter. "I've got them stowed away in the bag of grub; I'm steward, you know."

In passing up the river, Mark was much interested in watching the surrounding scenery, or rather the strange trees and various plants. It appeared to him to be a country of mangroves, and nothing else but mangroves; for the region of mud and slime is the peculiar kingdom of this singular tree. It seemed to take possession of the ground by its thousand roots that shoot out from its trunk, or by the long fibrous hair that hung down from the branches, and also by its numberless fruits which, before falling, send forth large roots, drop into the water by thousands, and are supported in an upright position by the weight of their roots, till they are at length carried by the tide to take possession of some new bank of mud. The mangroves rose at some parts of the river like an impenetrable bank of grayish verdure. Had it not been for the occasional sight of a beautiful kingfisher, a parrot, or a touraco, the sight of these gloomy mangroves would have proved very monotonous: but even their harsh notes were so scarce, that the repose of these solitudes was seldom disturbed.

Passing between the little islands of the Gaboon, it was some relief to come upon a canoe belonging to one of the mission-stations, and to exchange a hearty salute with them; and but for this circumstance, nothing happened to enliven the scene till they got further into the interior. It was a pleasure to find that here the aspect of nature changed considerably, and that the vegetation became more varied. Mark was interested in seeing the enimbas, a large kind of palm, which, Jack Maurice told him, though it did not produce much oil, was very useful as ready-made planks in the construction of their houses, and with shingles, which are easily prepared for the purpose of roofing.

"I should like very much to go on shore," said Mark to Jack. "I'd like to see how they build their houses."

THE MISSION-STATION CANOE.

"They don't build them at all," said Jack Maurice, laughing.

"Not build them," replied Mark; "why, then, what do they do?"

"They sew them. Every bit of a hut here away is sewn together bit by bit; a hammer and nail is not brought into use at all."

"Have you seen one done?" asked Mark, greatly interested.

"Oh yes; and since you are anxious to know, I'll build one right away," said Jack. "First," he continued, "you strip your planks. They are the branches, or rather the ribs, of the enimbas leaves, about eighteen feet in length, and very thick and narrow. They are quite level on the sides, and perfectly straight. The leaves are used in the place of tiles, and are ranged side by side, and fastened together by wooden pegs. The thread which they use is, of course, a fibre taken from another of the palm family, and is called *ojono*. It is easily bent, and is very strong. I think I have reason to remember that *ojono*. You see, boy, it is a species of what they call rotang-thorn. I was walking about the woods one day, helping that same old gentleman I told you about before, that went up Teneriffe, and all of a sudden something gripped me by the leg. I hollered out, and back came the old gentleman in no end of a hurry, to find out what was up, when there he found I was hard and fast caught by two hooks, like a great fish. That old gentleman told me lots of things, and when he had cut me free, explained to me that this was a rotang, and showed me it was armed with a kind of a bent hook, fastened in pairs on each side of the stalk, like the flukes of an anchor; and I can tell you they don't let you free so easily, if once they lay hold."

Mr. Sprent now ordered that the boat should be steered in the direction of a small cove, where they might rest and refresh themselves during the extreme heat of the day. Seizing this opportunity, Mark and Peter went strolling a little way into the interior, in the hope that they might be able to catch a parrot, or perhaps a young monkey; but, as it turned out, poor Peter caught a Tartar instead. He was poking his nose into the bushes, and peering cautiously into the trees, when all of a sudden his eyes lighted upon something like a bag made of leaves hanging at the end of a branch. In a moment Peter had pulled it off, and was proceeding to examine it more closely, when in a moment out flew a perfect shower of ants, most singular in their appearance, being large, light-coloured, and long-bodied. They swarmed round the head and face of the hapless Peter, inflicting a sharp and severe mark, and forcing both the boys to run back to their companions in as great a state of terror as if a dozen of savages were after them.

At this time they were also interested in watching a very remarkable red ant, close to the place where they were resting. Mr. Sprent discovered these creatures marching in close column through the grass, and it was evident they were observing a peculiar order of advance.

The division proceeded in two compact rows, being somehow entwined one with the other, so that the whole troop might have been raised at the end of a stick in masses. They had constructed also two long equal walls two or three inches in height, and equally distant the one from the other. Between these two walls a perfect stream of ants flowed on, carrying provisions or larvæ, which perhaps they had taken from some hostile republic. In the midst of those who were labouring so hard, were a number of large-headed ones, apparently directing the march. They carried no burdens; but they possessed a formidable pair of piercers, and were evidently the soldiers of the colony, and watched over its safety. They also acted as scouts on the flank of the double wall, collected the fugitives, urged on those who lagged behind, and repelled the attack of every enemy. Mark learned afterwards that great respect is paid to these travelling ants, and that they are very seldom molested by the natives;—indeed, they are somewhat superstitious about them, and when they encounter them they will pluck a leaf from the nearest tree and place it gently on the ground, thinking that this act will secure them against misfortune.

After some little delay, caused by their guide mistaking the way, they arrived at their destination. They first came upon a single hut, which proved to be the outpost of a village half hidden by the surrounding trees, and

A WARLIKE TRIBE.

which had thus been placed in a position of defence. To Mr. Sprent's surprise, he discovered he had come upon a warlike tribe, and not the people he had been in search of at all. A small hill, or rising ground, was speedily covered with a host of warriors, large and small;—children even rushed to join the company, brandishing weapons suited to their height, whilst in the centre stood the chief, carrying javelins and war-knives enough to stock a citadel. Mr. Sprent now left the boat in the keeping of the men, and taking Jack Maurice and the two lads, with the native interpreter, made signs that a canoe should be sent out to enable them to land.

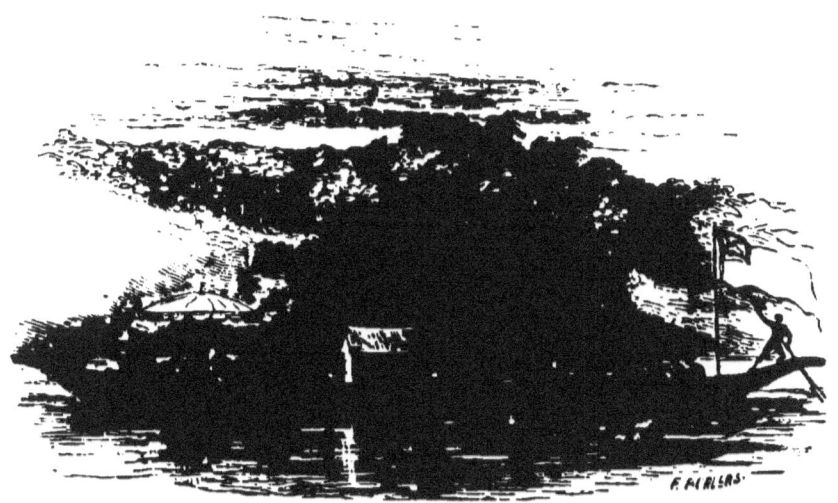

CANOE.

In a few minutes they had landed, and were in the presence of the chief. He was a man about forty, large, muscular, and hard-featured, with a projecting forehead, long lank arms, and his breast tattooed in a most disagreeable fashion. His only garment was the shaggy skin of some animal wrapped round his waist. He received them in a very stern and severe manner; but the eloquence of the interpreter, and the hope of obtaining presents, softened him in the end. Though the visit of the party was not expected, and though they had not come into actual contact with white people before, they appeared only half surprised, perhaps because they had heard something of the white men. Mr. Sprent hastened to distribute some tobacco-leaves amongst the company, which put them all into good-humour; and when a long-handled knife was added as the chief's " dash," they showed their formidable rows of filed teeth while smiling kindly upon them. The chief now invited Mr. Sprent and his little land-party to enter the village quite close at hand, which had more the appearance of a kind of fortress, having at each end of the wide street or double line of huts a rude guard-house.

While Mr. Sprent was occupied with the chief, Peter and Mark, in looking about them, discovered a Mussulman trader who had just arrived with a caravan from the interior. It was at once decided that Mark should begin to trade forthwith; and for this purpose he got some of his beads, and going to the place where the trader had taken up his temporary abode along with a young slave, presented the bunch of bright glass baubles.

PETER'S DISCOMFITURE. 87

THE MUSSULMAN TRADER.

Peter, who was hovering round the door to see that his friend was not imposed upon, was horrified to find that the Mussulman had quietly taken possession of the beads, and was making signs to our hero to be off about his business. "Why, that's cool, and no mistake," said Peter; "come, none of that,—if you don't give them beads up, you rascal, I'll make you remember it—you thief!"

To all these words, and many more besides, the trader turned a deaf ear, and the boys were forced to leave the beads in his hands, knowing that Mr. Sprent would not on any account stir up a quarrel for the sake of a few paltry beads, and might also forbid them to carry on their private speculations any further.

"I'll tell you what it is," said Peter, flourishing his hand above his head in a very determined manner: "we'll have nothing to do with them traders; we'll set to work among the natives themselves,—and my advice is, let's try the females."

It was arranged that they should return to their boat for the night, or rather that a small tent should be erected on the shore close to where the boat lay, and that they should "camp out" there. The chief was very anxious that Mr. Sprent and his small party should remain in the village; but having a strong prejudice against the natives, and fearing that they might attack his boat during the night, the mate declined the invitation. Seeing, however, that not only the chief but many of the warriors were by no means pleased at this arrangement, Mr. Sprent asked our hero to remain with Peter and the interpreter, to show that he was not afraid of them, but that his sole wish for retiring to his boat was that he might be in readiness to land the goods he had brought early next morning.

Both Mark and Peter were highly delighted, and with Mr. Sprent's permission were allowed to take their bags containing the things they wanted to barter with the natives. Fortunately, the interpreter had taken a fancy to both the lads, and also to Mark's small pocket-compass, which, at Peter's suggestion, was placed in Jack Maurice's hands, and the said Combo was informed that if he helped them to dispose of the other things they had, the compass was to be given to him for his " dash," or commission.

Under his escort the two boys made the tour of the village, and saw that this particular tribe of the Gaboon district were particularly skilful in the working of iron. They made great war-knives, and many short ones for various uses, along with adzes, and excellent hatchets of remarkable shape. One of these hatchets or knives represented the profile of a bird's head, set on a very arched neck which served for the handle; a groove divided the beak into two parts, while a hole was pierced to represent the eye. The blades were of good workmanship, and much better than those supplied to the natives by foreign merchants. They were also chased with ornamental devices, sometimes even inlaid with copper in a very tasteful manner. Their stock of tools surprised Mark by its simplicity. It consisted chiefly of two small portable anvils, one of them being fixed to the ground, whilst the other is used as a hammer. They heat the iron by a wood fire, which is kept alight by a double pair of bellows very ingeniously made. It is a piece of wood several inches in height, in which two parallel cavities are cut in the form of a cylinder, each of which is fitted at its extremity with a tube to convey the blast. Each of these cavities is covered with a very flexible skin, to which a wooden handle is fastened; and the covering, as it is alternately raised and lowered, draws in and gives out the air. These bellows, so simple and easy in their structure, Mark was informed by Mr. Sprent afterwards, are known over the whole of the African continent; and as for the strange bird-shaped knife, he was horrified to find it was used on sacrificial occasions. A single blow on the temple inflicts a mortal wound, and the bent part serves afterwards for the work of decapitation.

The most dangerous arm of this interesting but peculiar tribe, however, is the cross-bow, with which they shoot small poisoned arrows of bamboo. This weapon requires great strength on the part of the archer, to set it; but as it is discharged with a very slight pressure, it can be fired from the shoulder like a gun, and shoots with great precision. The bow, with its poisoned arrow, which is very deadly, is more used in the hunting-ground than on the battle-field; for the necessity of being seated in order to load the weapon makes it awkward in a struggle.

After the two boys had been through the village and had seen everything of consequence, they returned to the chief's dwelling. Tom-toms were speedily brought out, as well as other rude musical instruments, and the whole village began to dance. It was all Mark could do to keep Peter in order, for he laughed immoderately whenever he looked at any of the women ornamented with the *ito*, who had taken care to spread these appendages out to the utmost, so as to derive the proper fluttering motion. Two long rows of dancers, men and women, each conducted by a leader, wound about before the orchestra, followed and retreated from one another by turns, waxed more and more animated every moment, and were finishing with the most extraordinary gambols, when suddenly they were interrupted by hearing a great shout, and away ran every one to see what was the matter. Off ran Mark and Peter with the rest, when, after a time, they came upon two white men with guns. They were directing three negroes who were busily engaged in skinning a great serpent, two of them hauling at a rope fastened to the creature's neck, while a third was busily engaged cutting the dreadful creature open, which he did by sliding down its body as if it had been a pole.

The two serpent-hunters turned out to be Mr. Sprent and Jack Maurice, and so rejoiced were the natives at

A FORMIDABLE ENEMY.

SERPENT-HUNTING.

the death of such a formidable enemy, that the chief insisted they should turn back and be entertained by the whole tribe, the chief giving his wife up as a hostage for the safety of the boat and merchandise. There was certainly in nature nothing more formidable than this full-grown "puff adder." Mr. Sprent good-naturedly explained how he and Jack Maurice had come upon it with its body buried in the tawny soil.

"Was it quite covered up, sir?" said Mark.

"No, my boy," replied Mr. Sprent; "it had just left its flat, cruel-looking head lying on the ground, and free from sand. It lay very steady, confident in its deadly power, with a most malignant glare in its eyes; but with all its terrible venom, we had a more deadly one for it."

"Did you shoot it, sir?"

"Shoot it!—not at all. Who would waste good powder and shot on such a villain?"

"Then how did you kill it—with a lasso? I know Jack can use it," said Mark.

"Well, my boy, I'll not puzzle you any more. What will you say if I tell you we killed it with a little tobacco juice?"

"With tobacco juice, sir; that is indeed very strange. How did you manage it?"

"Well, we rubbed some of the tobacco oil on a stick. Fortunately, Jack had a pipe as old as the hills, which turned out a good deal of oil, and while he made the villain bite the stick, I squirted a lot of juice in its face, and in a very short time he was dead."

"Is this serpent very poisonous, sir?" said Mark.

"It is so—very; and they are more dreaded by the natives than almost any other of the numerous poisonous snakes of Africa. This mainly comes from its indolent nature. Other snakes, more active, will move rapidly away upon the approach of man; but the puff adder will frequently lie still, either too lazy to move, or dozing beneath the warm sun. Its broad, ace of clubs-shaped head, its thick body and suddenly tapered tail, and its checkered back, are all evidences of its poisonous nature."

"Why do they call it a puff adder?" inquired Mark.

"Because it has a practice of puffing out, or swelling the body, when irritated," replied Mr. Sprent. "But what is this?" he said, drawing Mark's attention to a group of natives, who were evidently in a state of excitement about something extraordinary. They had been walking up together from the place where the serpent had been killed to the village during the above conversation, and Mark had not observed that Peter was not with them.

Drawing near, they discovered that it was none other than that incorrigible young individual who was the cause of all the howling, screaming, and yelling. He had taken this opportunity of exhibiting one of his dolls, and as it opened and shut its eyes, the natives were wild in their expressions of admiration at it. Peter kept calling out, "Moondah, moondah! fetich, great fetich!" every time he did so giving a pull to the wire, which either jerked the eyes open or shut. In a very short time the chief of the village heard of it, and came out to see this wonder-fetich for himself. By the help of the interpreter, Peter was giving the chief to understand that "for a consideration" it might become his. They were in the act of negotiation when Mr. Sprent and Mark came up, and as Peter did not see them, they kept out of sight to see how the matter would end.

The chief offered some knives, and then some pearls; but Peter shook his head, and pointed to a massive bracelet made of gold upon one of the arms of his wife.

"I must say he is not modest," said Mr. Sprent; "why, that bracelet might be a fortune to him." The chief hesitated; but seeing this, the wily Peter drew out the other doll, which was made of wood and jointed, and bending its legs and arms into all sorts of shapes, offered it into the bargain. This proved irresistible, and they were carried away in state to the fetich hut, and placed amongst the other grotesque figures there; Peter having got the bracelet in return.

"Oh, Mr. Sprent," said Mark, " Peter ought not to be allowed to cheat the savages; he must have made them believe these dolls were gods."

"Well, I don't think they will worship them," said Mr. Sprent, laughing, not being so scrupulous as our hero. "They are very fond of any figure resembling a European, and though they do not exactly worship them, so far as I know, they are very fond of having them. If Peter had not brought these dolls, it would have made no difference, for everything there is fetich."

"But do they worship nothing, then?" asked Mark.

"I can scarcely say they do," said Mr. Sprent. "They

have a certain fear regarding the wandering spirits of the dead; and they believe in the existence of genii, as possessing great power in inflicting evil. They have an implicit belief in the virtue of a multitude of talismans; and of fetiches, which they suppose possess the power of preserving them from sickness, or from the accidents of war. The little ornament of tiger's claws, which the women wear round their necks, is called *moondah;* the finely-cut plate on their fishing tackle is called the same; and so is the little particle of burnt ashes of a leopard's brain, which the warrior hides under his cotton drawers, and grasps at the moment of battle to give him courage. This is regarded as a very powerful fetich, but there is one more powerful still."

As Mr. Sprent stopped, and looked smilingly at Mark, apparently wishing to be asked what this extraordinary thing was, Mark was not long in gratifying him. "They are certainly a very queer race," he said. "Will Peter's dolls be more powerful than the leopard's brain?"

"No, not half so powerful, my boy," said Mr. Sprent; "what do you say to the ashes from the burnt flesh or bones of a white man!"

"Oh, how dreadful!" said Mark, shuddering. "I wonder they don't burn us up at once, then, as that might supply a whole tribe."

"They won't do any such thing, my boy," said Mr.

Sprent; "they are beginning, even away up in the interior, to dread the name of a white man, and are too anxious to trade with him for the things they value so highly. It is a pity our ship could not have got up this river; for we should have driven a brisk trade here, and got home all the sooner."

"Is it likely we shall stay much longer here, sir?" said Mark eagerly.

"Do you mean the boat, or the *Stratton?* I expect, so far as we are concerned, to be away very soon; for we have not brought the kind of things they value very highly. They are great hunters, and it is guns they prize most; but I dare say we shall get our cargo disposed of, for they have just had a grand elephant hunt, before we arrived, and the chief tells the interpreter he has some large tusks."

"So, then, we go home after that, sir, at any rate!" said Mark.

"No, my boy; we sail directly for Old Calabar. It will be a relief, at all events, to get out into blue water once more, if only for a short time."

CHAPTER V.

PRIVATE TRADERS.

THE next day, the merchandise was brought up to the village, when a brisk trade commenced; Mr. Spreat conducting it on the "round" system,—namely, putting out one of every article, from a needle to a gun. As it had only been a matter of speculation on the part of the captain, who had been told a native trading-place existed already, they had only small, light articles with them, such as beads, small looking-glasses, tobacco and pipes, worsted caps, flints, knives, and a few guns.

When Mr. Spreat had disposed of everything, Jack Maurice kindly took in hand to assist Mark with his bag of articles, each of which produced much merriment amongst the crew of the *Stratton's* boat, when it was displayed.

"By all that's comical, boy, what possessed you to bring a horse-shoe?" said one of the men.

"And he was right, and showed his sense," said Maurice; "aren't the darkies fond of charms and such like; and don't we nail up a horse-shoe to the foremast ourselves afore we go a voyage? It's worth all their fetiches put together!"

"That's true," said another; "but then, how are you to get them darkies to know that? They have never seen a British ship, very likely; our boat has been the largest thing of the kind that has come their way. It strikes me, they don't use their canoes very much, leastways they don't seem to be good at handling them!"

"No; because they have come from the interior," said Jack; "but I'll tell you what we'll do: Como shall tell them we use a horse-shoe to frighten away evil spirits from our ships, or to insure good luck during the voyage. I was forgetting, Master Como bound himself to help you lads in the matter; has the rascal not kept his word?"

"Oh, we were interrupted by you and the mate killing that brute of a serpent," said Peter; "but for that matter, he hasn't troubled his head about us further than by taking us through the village; for he fell in with a sweet young creature of a darkie, and he's been a galiwanting with her ever since."

"Then he has forgot the compass, boy," said Maurice; "but not a word of it till after we get the goods disposed of."

When Como fairly understood what was required of him, he entered into the business with great spirit, saying, "Ya, ya, me see; leab it to me, me get gold-dust for dis 'ere."

Disappearing with the horse-shoe, carefully rolled in a bright-coloured handkerchief, they waited to see the result; and very soon after, a native, who stood next in rank to the chief, came back with him to hold a grand palaver about it. He offered knives and pearls, and all sorts of native produce; but Como gave him to understand that nothing but gold would do in this case, knowing that Mark could not stow away a great elephant's tusk. The prime minister seemed to be near his wit's end, when Jack Maurice turned to walk away to the boat, carrying the coveted treasure with him, and he at once bade the interpreter ask Jack to give him a few minutes to consider whether he could get the gold-dust or not. After a good deal of running backwards and forwards on the part of the prime-minister, an amicable arrangement was come to, in which Mark's horse-shoe became the property of the king; and he in return the happy possessor of a small bag of gold-dust. As it was late, it was decided to postpone the business till next morning; but before that time arrived they were forced to leave in a desperate hurry, barely escaping with their lives.

The confusion was caused by Como having eloped with the dark girl through the night, and by some means or other the circumstance became known, when the angry father and still angrier betrothed,—an immense and dreadfully formidable-looking fellow,—went off in pursuit of the fugitives. The indignation of the whole tribe was roused; and had it not been for the carefulness of Mr. Sprent, who had insisted upon a good watch being kept night and day, they might all have been murdered while they slept. As it was, they had difficulty in getting the boat off before the natives were upon them with knives and tomahawks, yelling and shrieking like demons.

"If Master Como turns up again, and I come athwart him," said Jack Maurice, "I'll give him something he won't forget in a hurry, for the fright he has given us."

"It's my impression he is hidden in one of the huts in the village," said Mr. Sprent, wiping the moisture from his forehead, as they rested on their oars beyond the reach of the natives.

"Then if so be's that that's the case, sir," said Long Jack, grinning, "he'll never hact as interpreter again. I'd have thought twice before I hinterfered with that savage's sweetheart; did you see the gentleman's teeth, —ain't they sharp-filed?"

"Ain't they!" said Peter, shuddering, and pretending to be dreadfully afraid. "I hope we won't see them, or rather feel the strength of them on our bodies."

They were startled at this moment by hearing a loud shout and then a groan of agony, and Mr. Sprent at once ordered the boat to be rowed with caution towards the part of the bank from whence the noise had proceeded. What was their astonishment to find the unhappy fugitive Como, stripped naked, and tied to a post.

"It would serve him out to give him a good fright," said Mr. Sprent; "come, lads, pull for that clear space on the opposite side; we'll have our dinner there before we set the fellow at liberty."

"If I may make so free, sir," said Maurice, "it would be better to keep by this side; for the water is shallow there, and by the nature of the vegetation I should say it would be a good place for a lion or an alligator to hide in."

The men having received orders to pull, Mr. Sprent took Maurice's advice, and steered past the place where Como was tied, paying no attention to his howls and yells, till they were fairly round the projecting point, when they landed, and "all hands" were despatched to collect wood for a fire. When they had managed to light it, Long Jack, who had gone to take a peep at Como, and also to see that no natives were in the neighbourhood, now returned, and being a kind-hearted man, begged that the unfortunate interpreter should be set at liberty; "for," he said, "if you keep him much longer, he'll go out of his mind; and what makes me more sorry for the poor wretch is, they have gone and shaved off his wool, and left him with a poll as bare as Peter's old captain's was."

COMO AT LIBERTY. 103

LIGHTING A FIRE.

Mr. Sprent at once agreed to this, and Como was set at liberty, being brought back by Peter and Baba, a boy belonging to the mission station, in great triumph. While they rested, Como amused them by relating how he had managed to escape, and then how he had been captured, which caused much merriment, especially when it came out that he had not been content with carrying off the girl, but had managed to get the household furniture, such as it was, of her betrothed, and his canoe into the bargain.

"It's a wonder to see you alive, Como," said Mark; "I cannot understand how he let you off so easily."

"Easy!" cried Como, "and him took my har, and mine clothes, and mine all things!"

"Be thankful he didn't bite the life out of you with them teeth of his," said Peter; "but perhaps he means to come back and finish you slick off after he gets the gal and the goods safely stowed."

This idea was so dreadful to poor Como, that nothing would satisfy him but they must set off at once; and it was only when they reached the side of the *Stratton*, and he found himself safely on the deck once more, that he seemed to breathe in a natural manner. Peter was constantly playing some joke upon him, such as shouting out that he saw several canoes, and warlike men standing in the bows; and he kept appealing to Mark if he did not notice one especially, who appeared to be sharpening a long row of white teeth.

"Me stay at the station again," said poor Como,

"me go no more expeditions; hate black fellows,—all rascals."

Every one had laughed at this remark of Como's, for though he was a half-caste by birth, he was blacker than many of the natives of the Gaboon; but he insisted that, as his father had been an Englishman, he was entitled to consider himself a "white man" also, regardless of his colour, which was certainly against him.

A few days afterwards, the cheering news was passed round that the *Stratton* was to weigh anchor that afternoon, when she would proceed to the trading stations in the district of the Cameroons. The dull routine of the daily duties, the broiling sunshine by day, and the chilling rain by night, was enough to quench any amount of energy; and even Peter, the life of the *Stratton's* crew, began to hang his head in rather a dispirited manner. As for Mark, he more than once found himself longing for home and his old life there, for he felt himself reduced to a machine—to pull, to let go, to eat, to sleep, to wake again. But great was the excitement, and cheering the bustle, when all hands turned up to prepare the ship for sea; it was surprising how even the fever-stricken ones ran or shuffled about the deck, lending their small but willing aid.

The *Stratton* now cleared the land, and after making the first mouth of the five rivers of Beas, stood in to resume trade in that quarter, where numerous opportunities for barter were to be found; the leading object being, however, to fill up with palm-oil, which was abundant in that quarter.

The blacks here were of a tribe apparently disposed to peaceful avocations, and for the most part engaged in turning the soil to account. The manufacture of palm-oil had been carried on to a considerable extent, and stores of this commodity had been laid up to wait the arrival of the first trading ship; consequently, an active scene of barter now went on with the *Stratton*, though she had to be on her guard against frequent tricks on the part of the dealers. One of these was to produce large calabashes and jars seemingly full of the pure oil; but, in fact, only containing it at the top, by means of a false bottom, the contents underneath consisting of nothing but water. The captain and mate were far too old stagers to be thus deceived into a loss of several shillings on each cask.

During this time an incident occurred producing a lively idea of the nature of the country, with the dangers to which life in Africa is exposed. Two women were returning from their work in the fields, the one leading a little child by the hand, when all at once a huge lion, who had been lying in ambush at the foot of a small clump of trees, sprang out, and seizing hold of the child, made off with it to a part of the jungle. The women were so bewildered, that they stood for a few moments transfixed with horror; but when the lion had got half-way across

LYING IN AMBUSH.

the clearing, they set up a great shout, and ran with all their might towards the jetty, which was not far distant. Fortunately, a good many of the natives were assembled there at the time; and when the captain of the *Stratton* heard what had happened, he at once gave orders that half of the crew should proceed to the rescue of the unfortunate child. Armed with guns and pistols, and a few carrying cutlasses, they were not long in reaching the place where the women had seen the lion disappear. Forming themselves into an organized band under the charge of Mr. Sprent and Long Jack, they boldly encircled the clump of jungle the lion was hiding in, and while Peter and Mark volunteered to climb a tree to see if they could observe him in that fashion, every one stood silent and almost breathless.

Suddenly they heard a faint wail, as if from the stolen child, and it was with difficulty the mother could be made to restrain herself, or held back from rushing in to save it at the risk of both their lives. Mark was the first to appear, when he stated that the lion was lying at the end of an open space, about a yard away from the child, and that his strong impression was that the brute could easily be shot, provided he continued to lie in the same position. Unfortunately, at this part all the strong trees had been cut down, and it was considered almost impossible that one could be found strong enough to bear the weight of any but a boy; and the natives were quite unskilled in the use of fire-arms.

"I see no way for it," said Mr. Sprent, "but to trust to you, Mark. Do you think you could take a steady aim? It will be better to get the brute out, at any rate; we will then have a better chance to get a shot at him in the open field."

Very proud was Mark, when, with the captain's gun in his hands, he crept cautiously back to the wood again, which when he had reached, he found to his great delight that the lion had evidently fallen asleep, and had turned his head in a better direction for a shot. At that moment Peter, who had been swinging from branch to branch like a monkey, suddenly lost his footing, and came crashing through the trees close to where the lion was lying. Up he sprang with an angry growl, that made more than the hapless Peter's heart quake, and was about to spring upon him, when Mark, taking as steady an aim as he possibly could, fired. Out rushed the lion, apparently unhurt, and in the confusion Mark fancied he must have shot Peter instead, to judge by the yelling and groaning that followed. But the lion had been wounded, and very severely too, and after staggering about for a minute, uttering deep groans and growls, Mr. Sprent, with the help of Long Jack, soon finished him by firing several charges into him.

"You have done well, my boy," said Mr. Sprent to Mark as they stood together by the carcass of the dying animal. "See, this is where your shot struck, just below his ear; a very good shot indeed. Did you practise much at home?"

"Not with a gun, sir," said Mark; "but one of the boys had a large revolver—it had six chambers in it—and we used to practise firing at an old door, where we drew a circle with chalk."

"Ah," said Mr. Sprent, laughing, "I've tried that sort of thing myself, and very good sport we made of it too."

Peter had been dragged out of the bush where he had fallen into, and after a good deal of talking was persuaded he was not in the least hurt, with the exception of a few scratches. The child, too, seemed to have been stunned with terror, more than anything else, and was carried away in the arms of her delighted mother. When the lion had been skilfully skinned by some of the natives, Mr. Sprent ordered one of the men to take it on board, and as they were passing along the path, he turned to Mark, who was close behind him, and said, "Won't your mother be pleased when you lay that down for a hearth-rug!"

"O sir," said Mark, "am I really to get the skin; is that what you mean?"

"Of course," said Mr. Sprent; "haven't you the best right to it?"

"If I may make so bold, sir," said Peter, "I think I deserve a piece of the skin, for I've had more to bear than Mark has, though I wasn't so lucky as to shoot him exactly."

"No, it's not likely," said Mr. Sprent; "I have a notion you'd make tracks out of the way of a kangaroo, if it gave a jump at you."

"Well, sir, I think you would have jumped too, if you had seen the horrid glare, like fire, a-coming out of them dreadful eyes, and heard the roar close to your very ears, —it was enough to make your hair stand on end."

"That's to say if you had hair," said Mark; "there was no danger of yours doing anything of the kind, for it's rather of the woolly order."

That same afternoon, two man-of-war boats came alongside the *Stratton*, and the two officers in command came on board. It turned out they were in search of a slaver, which was supposed to be lying at anchor in a bight of the river, but would not embark her slaves for several days. The natives at that part were supposed to be not only savage, but given to all sorts of villany; and as this was the first time English vessels of war had visited these waters, it was thought that a demonstration to show the power of England would have a good effect upon the natives in favour of future traders. The captain of the *Stratton*, accordingly, gladly promised any assistance in his power, and ordered a strict watch to be kept on deck.

The evening had now set in, and heavy clouds gave promise of a gloomy night; the men had stowed themselves away as best they could, and all, save the look-out, were fast asleep; while the officers were keeping it up with the captain and mates in the cabin.

The wind roared through the rigging, the rain fell incessantly in one continuous stream, and flash and peal came quicker on one another. The glimmering of

WATCHING THE SLAVER.

the cabin lamp was lost amidst the flaring of the lightning, which one moment lit up with the light of day, the next left a pitchy darkness. At the first flash, Mr. Herbert, the captain of the man-of-war's cutter, rushed to the ladder and scrambled on deck, hallooing for the watch and for the *Stratton's* crew, as if the command of the *Stratton* had passed into his hands entirely.

For the first five or six minutes he shouted for his pistols and for his cutlass, calling upon each of his officers, but with little or no effect. The truth being, they were dead asleep on the cabin floor. It then gradually dawned upon him that "the freshes," which is similar to the bore in India, was soaring past, causing the vessel to groan at her anchor. At every flash could be seen the startled stragglers endeavouring to scramble aft, at their wit's end to avoid coming in contact with the empty casks which were pitching and rolling about the deck. And now a new danger beset them, for the brig, being only half-laden, rolled so heavily that it was feared she would turn keel up.

In this emergency, the men who had collected aft were kept staggering from side to side; as she heeled over to starboard, "Larboard side," was shouted, and away they went, at the imminent risk of being crushed. Scarcely had they succeeded in reaching the bulwarks, when the vessel recovered herself and rolled over to port. "Starboard side," roared Mr. Herbert and Mr. Sprent together, who had now come on deck, and back again they ran; doing this for nearly two hours, till the tornado had passed, and the commotion of the waters had subsided.

In the scramble, poor Peter had been rescued from an awkward position, where he lay heels up jammed amongst some casks. "Oh," he shouted, or rather groaned, "it all comes o' me deceiving them poor darkies about them dolls; they've let their evil spirit get me! I'll have no more to do with them dolls! I wish I'd taken Mark's advice, greenhorn though he be!"

When dragged out by Jack Maurice and Mark, he mistook his rescuers for naked savages going to eat him; and, consequently, was preparing to sell his life as dearly as he could, when a flash of lightning revealed the faces of his shipmates. "Blow me, but I was a-thinking I was to be cooked and eaten, or *wisy wersa*, as the captain says."

"Come, you sea-lawyer ye, stand on your own pins," said Jack Maurice. "I've enough to do to steady myself. But what was that you were saying about a doll, and cheating honest darkies?"

"You shut up, Jack, and don't tell tales out o' school; besides, a man ain't responsible for his figures o' speech when his keel is uppermost."

"He was crying for a dollie to play with—wasn't he now, Mark!" said Maurice, laughing; "pretty little dear," and Maurice chucked him under the chin.

From that time, till the end of the voyage, poor Peter went under the name of Dollie Darkie, to his intense disgust.

The daylight dawned upon a dismal scene: a cold, drizzling rain hid the land like a fog, and the unwholesome vapours from the shore gave to the air a feeling of infection, which made one think of fever and ague; and, consequently, every one was as dull and spiritless as possible. Mr. Herbert called his men together without delay; and up they came, rubbing their bruised heads and limbs, and growling like a lot of angry bears. The *Stratton's* boat was got in readiness to accompany the man-of-war boats, and they shoved off and made for up the river. As they progressed, the shores appeared even more thickly wooded than at the entrance, which screened them from the rays of the sun, that a little before noon began to blaze out and disperse the mists of the morning. The solitude of the woods was enlivened by a variety of birds; while parrots and paroquets, with their shrill and odious screams, were flying overhead, their brilliant plumage contrasting with the shrubs and colour of the scenery.

A little after noon, the boats were run in-shore, and all hands were permitted to land and rest. Mark and Peter, accompanied by a boy belonging to the man-of-war boats, called Layton, set out at once to search for cocoa-nuts, which they were not long in discovering. Layton at once scrambled up the trees and pitched the fruit down to Mark and Peter, ordering them to take them to the men at a little distance off.

"I say, Mark," said Peter, "I don't like this bordering-about son of a middy. I wote that we go off on our own hook, and leave him to carry his own nuts."

"Well, I don't mind if I do," said Mark; "he does give himself airs; and he's younger than we are. We'll let him see, that though he can order about the men belonging to his boat, he can't order us."

Accordingly, when they had carried the next load of nuts to the men, they started off in the opposite direction, after they had explained to Jack Maurice "their little game." Going more into the interior, they came upon a

GATHERING COCOA-NUTS.

GATHERING COCOA-NUTS.

whole colony of monkeys leaping from bough to bough, and staring at them with chattering wonder.

"I'd like to catch one o' them young ones," said Peter. "I've sort o' set my heart upon taking back a monkey to a little girl what stays in a little shop in Bristol. She axed me to do it, and I'd like to keep my word, if possible."

"I daresay we can manage that," said Mark, laughing.

"And how is it to be done? Shall I go back and get Long Jack's gun?"

"Not unless you want to have a dead one. Look here," said Mark, and he pulled a red handkerchief from his pocket, and fastening it to the end of the branch of a tree, drew Peter behind a bush; "you watch that side, and I shall take this," he said, "and I shall be much mistaken if one of these monkeys don't fall into a trap."

In a few minutes, first one large monkey and then another came swinging down to have a peep at the bright red object, followed by a troop of little ones, who elbowed each other, and chattered and cried, in their eagerness to get a good view. One very small one, but evidently full of spirit and daring, ran along a branch of the tree close above where the handkerchief was fastened; and, while the other monkeys applauded, he hooked his tail on to the branch and let himself hang down so as to catch hold of the handkerchief with his claws. When too late, he discovered his arms were not quite long enough, and before he could swing himself back again, Mark had pitched his jacket over him, which he had stripped off for the purpose, and had him secure in his hands.

"Well, now, but that was neatly done," said Peter admiringly; "however did you learn to catch monkeys?"

"Oh, out of the books you laugh at me for reading," said Mark. "Have you never heard that monkeys are about the most curious and prying animals in existence?"

"No, I never heard that," said Peter; "but I wish I could catch another. I am afraid, though, they've all taken fright."

"Well, never mind," said Mark; "you don't want two, and I make you a present of this one upon the condition you help me, first opportunity, to catch a young parrot."

This Peter cordially promised to do, and the two worthies returned to show their prize to their companions.

CHAPTER VI.

WATCHING THE SLAVER.

WHEN the men had rested sufficiently, they set out again, pulling and sailing alternately, singing as they went, till dusk. Many canoes had been noticed towards the close of the day, although only one had been boarded; the people who belonged to her, on the boat's approaching, jumped overboard and swam ashore, dreading the jaws of an alligator less than close contact with a white man. A supply of yams, bananas, and roasted corn was obtained from the deserted canoe, and some articles were deposited as payment.

Mr. Herbert sought out a snug creek where he might lie for a day or two undiscovered, and from whence he could pounce upon the Spanish slaver as she shipped her slaves. This having been found, boughs were cut and distributed to form a screen for the boats, and every precaution taken to prevent discovery; such as cooking only by dusk, keeping the men within bounds, and forbidding the use of fire-arms. However, amusements were not wanting; there was bathing, the number of bathers being a security against attack from alligators, who were so frightened that they were glad to get out of the way. They succeeded in getting a supply of yams from the adjoining swamp; also in taking a few fish, which were cooked for the officers. On the evening of the second day one of the officers was despatched by Mr. Herbert with two Kroomen in the canoe, armed with a musket, and wrapped in his blanket-frock and trousers. Silently they sped over the water till they approached the slaver, when they glided noiselessly round her, almost coming in contact with a large canoe which just then left her side and went paddling to the shore. The Kroomen urged their small canoe under the slaver's stern, and as they drew near voices could be distinguished in the cabin. The officer stood up and managed to reach the sills of the cabin-window: telling the men to keep the canoe steady, he raised himself by his hands till he could see into the cabin. There sat the captain, with his first and second officers, with pistols before them; also several natives, the most conspicuous of whom wore a cocked hat, a marine officer's dingy dress-coat and epaulettes, a cavalry sword, and a white shirt which reached half-way to his knees, while his legs and feet were bare.

This was evidently the redoubtable King Jacket, and

the others were members of his court: some had striped shirts on; some only a waistcoat; but none wore trousers. They were full of importance; and, by the earnestness of their conversation, it was evident they were concluding a bargain. Quietly the officer lowered himself down, and returned to the boats, not without feeling thankful, no doubt, that he had escaped unhurt. It was concluded that the slaves would be embarked about midnight; and, consequently, Mr. Herbert determined upon paying the slaver a visit. The boats were not long preparing, and the pinnace pushed out, leaving the cutter and the *Stratton's* boat to follow. After pulling for some time, and steering for a particular light, which was intercepted by a dark body, it proved to be the slaver. "Give alongside, and five dollars to the first man who boards!" shouted Mr. Herbert. The boat sheered alongside, the promised reward doing more to create confusion than an eighteen-pound shot would have done. Instead of the oars being tossed, they were jerked in anyhow; the bowman, instead of holding on with the hook until the boat was fast, simply held till the boat was alongside, and scrambled into the slaver's chains; the efforts of the others to get up the side pushed the boat off, and the current hurried her astern. Mr. Herbert was at no time famed for command of temper, now he was perfectly outrageous; the boat had dropped so far astern that it was a full quarter of an hour before she again got alongside. The boat-hook was still hanging to the chain-plates, and by its side was the unfortunate bowman, nearly exhausted, endeavouring to hide himself from the slaver's crew, who were apparently in the utmost consternation.

The hold was ransacked, but no slaves could be found. Everything was in apparent readiness, however: the slave-deck laid, the platform rigged over the side; even the tubs, which are only used in slave-ships, were on deck. But, as there were no Africans on board, it was useless to think of seizing her, as an action of damages might be brought against the captors. Mr. Herbert, therefore, was forced reluctantly to give her up; and, as the time allowed for the expedition was nearly ended, they returned without further delay to their ship.

Some days after, the *Stratton's* cargo of palm-oil being shipped, she set sail, to the delight of every one on board, for old England. On passing the mouth of one of the rivers, they sighted the sloop-of-war, *Psyche*, and observed that her boats were engaged firing into a large canoe that was attempting to make its escape up one of the tributaries. Maurice gave it as his opinion that this must be one of the slaver's boats that had been sent down to spy if the coast was clear, and had been observed. Whether this was the case or not, Mark never discovered; and, indeed, his thoughts were so full of home, and what they would all say to him on his return, that he did not take the amount of interest in the

FIRING ON THE SLAVER'S BOAT.

fate of the slaver that he would have done at another time.

As the ship glided along almost imperceptibly, yet getting over the sea wonderfully well, Mark and Peter took up their position in the tops, for the sake of having a last glimpse of the coast before it faded from their sight for ever.

"Holloa!" shouted Peter, "what's that on the horizon? A boat with a signal hoisted!"

Mark strained his eyes in the direction Peter pointed, and came to the same conclusion, when he immediately hailed the deck.

No time was lost in bearing down for the boat, which proved to have escaped from a wreck four days before. There were six men on board of it, all in the utmost state of distress and misery from want of food and water, having had neither the one nor the other since they left the ship. They were quickly hoisted on board, and had their wants supplied, and in a few days were quite able to assist the *Stratton's* crew in the discharge of their duty.

With the exception of this incident, nothing occurred to break the usual monotonous routine of their life on shipboard. The weather was favourable in the extreme, and after a very quick passage the *Stratton* reached the Bristol Channel one breezy morning, got her pilot, and beat up to the King's Roads, where a tug brought her speedily up the river into the well-known old port, crowded with shipping, and alive with the usual stir.

HELP IN SIGHT.

Then came the bustle of warping in to her berth, amidst the " Yo heave ho!" of the crew, and the excitement on the wharves. Mark felt proud, as well as full of emotion; for it brought strangely to mind the time when he used, as a mere school-boy, to look at the foreign vessels coming in from distant regions: the sailors with great broad-leaved straw hats, all with something in their hand for shore—tropical birds and fruits, calabashes, monkeys, rude wooden carvings, which they had bartered for a clasp-knife or a string of beads. And here it was all realized, with himself as one of the jovial party, and his own actual recollections to go back upon. He had many curiosities to take home—among them a gorgeous parrot, in a cage which Long Jack had made for him; and it may well be believed that he made the best of his way for the dear old door, bounding up the stair, at the top of which he was clasped in his mother's arms, while his brothers danced about him in the wildest ecstacies.

Many happy days passed by, during which Mark enjoyed the delight of being at home again to the fullest degree. By day he roved through the streets with his brothers and their companions—sometimes accompanied by his shipmate Peter—often telling them stories of his adventures; and at night it was still pleasanter sitting with his mother for one of the hearers. Bristol, however, was not a place where one who had tasted the excitement of a sailor's life could long bear to be idle; Mark began to be restless, and though he had no wish to try the African coast again, he was bent on carrying out the profession. It so happened that his uncle, Captain John Price, had been appointed to the command of a fine ship bound for China, belonging to the same owners as the *Stratton*, and this circumstance decided our hero's course, for his uncle was enabled to offer him a berth as first-class boy on board the *Flamborough*.

A good departure was made down Channel, and the ship made a rapid passage down the Atlantic without anything particular occurring. She rounded the Cape of Good Hope in rough weather, but escaped disaster of any kind, after which she made her way through the Indian Ocean very much in the same fortunate manner; the incidents being all of the nature which skilful captains approve, though scarcely worth mentioning in the way of adventure. So accurate had been the course steered, that the first land sighted was one of the Nicobar Islands, towards the mouth of the Straits of Malacca, into which the *Flamborough* duly entered, and might then be said to be fairly on the beaten way for China. Here the real difficulties of the voyage commenced, as the danger in navigating these straits is great. They had constantly to be on the look-out for treacherous shoals and sharp reefs of coral; in addition to which there was the necessity of caution against piratical proas and other suspicious craft. Many of these were seen, both in the distance and near at hand; but the *Flamborough* being too big for them, they were content as yet merely to hover about her and stand away again, not quite liking the appearance of her long guns and carronades. The small arms were always kept ready to welcome such guests, and they would have found a few hearts of oak prepared to give them a warm reception, had they tried boarding. Such troubles were almost fully made up for by the novelties continually presented, in every shape of which tropical shores are capable. Every now and then the shore was in view, where the scenery was wildly beautiful; now luxuriantly wooded to the very water's edge, and now running up into magnificent mountains. The odd thing was, too, that while these far surpassed anything Mark had conceived for oddity, at the same time he was always feeling familiar with them, as if he had seen them before. He could not help fancying that he knew the odd little Chinese pilot—with a tail to his head, and his toes curled up, and bright-coloured clothes—who took the ship up

PENINSULA OF SHAN-TSAY.

to Whampoa; and as to the first junk he saw near the land, singular as it looked in its antiquated style, still it was exactly what he had expected.

Whampoa is the anchorage for large vessels going up

the Si-Kiang or Tigris river on the way to Canton, from which large city it is distant about ten miles; a very heavy pull for the boats of the various ships on their way up to town. Here a Chinese compradore, a most essential character to every European ship, took charge of the *Flamborough* in all matters of general business: and a very funny individual he was, with his long fingernails like bird's claws; his variety of petticoats; and his pigeon English, which made Mark think of a child talking. The anchors were no sooner down than myriads of native beggars surrounded the new ship, floating on all sorts of articles, from a sanpan or river-boat to a plank, or even a couple of bladders joined together. Among these an old Chinese woman appeared in a kind of dingey or canoe with a hood, accompanied by five or six little native children, from three to eight years of age. When they came alongside, they sang out in pigeon English, "Beef-war, soup-war!"

The steward fetched them a bone that had been well polished before, whereupon the old woman cried out in great disdain, "All bone-war—no good war—want beef-war!" tapping the children on the stomachs all the time to point out their emptiness, though they were really very fat, chubby little creatures. The children were so well trained in their parts, that they did their best to make their stomachs look as empty as possible, in corroboration of the old woman's statement.

"Me jump overboard, you throw me one bottley," screamed one of the little urchins.

The steward allowed Mark to go to his pantry for one, and when it was pitched over into the water, three of the little children, scarcely able to walk, jumped into the river to secure the prize, which is a much coveted one. As soon as the bottle had been thrown, the old woman flung pieces of wood into the water, which the children seized and stuck under their arms, paddling away after the coveted treasure. When the successful one had returned to the boat, the woman patted him most affectionately, in token of her approval; but when the others returned empty-handed, she cuffed them soundly till they screamed.

"O you female monster!" cried the good-natured steward; "you shall have no beef-war for your cruelty. Did you expect the whole three to get the bottle? Be off with you, I say."

At Whampoa the great river divides into several branches, flowing steadily, the country being luxuriant on either side, with a dazzling sky, that allowed but little to be seen around. Midway, however, ran what is called the Pearl Stream, leading to Canton, where everything connected with the cargo had to be done; and as Mark was able to make one of a boat's crew when the captain went up to the factories, it was not long before his time came for enjoying the sights in this way.

AN INTERVIEW.

No sooner had they got to their destination, than, to Mark's intense delight, Captain Price put aside his

ENTRANCE TO THE RIVER LEADING TO CANTON.

"captain's face" and manner, and became the jovial Uncle John of memorable days in Bristol. "Well, my boy," he said as Mark entered the cabin, having been requested to go to the captain by the steward; "how have you been getting along during the voyage?—comfortable, I hope!"

"Oh yes, sir," replied Mark in a tone of deference, as he still stood somewhat in awe of the captain; "I like coming to China better than going to Africa, sir."

"Why, how's this—two sirs in one sentence?" said Captain Price, laughing; "come, come, my boy, give us your hand, now that we are in port. I'm not the captain except before strangers or during the hours of duty; I am old Uncle John, mind that." Seeing that Mark was a little overcome, he added hastily, "I'm going up to the factories this afternoon, how would you like to go with me?"

"Oh, I should like to go very much indeed," said Mark, with brightening eyes.

"Very well, we shall get Mr. Sutton to let you off from your watch. Upon the whole, he has given me a favourable account of you during the cruise, and now we must have a sort of a holiday together."

"Oh, how kind of you, Uncle John!" replied Mark gratefully. "Do you know, I almost wished I had gone in another ship at the beginning of the voyage, for Mr. Sutton was so severe. I think he was harder upon me, because I was your nephew, than upon the other boys."

"Very likely," said the captain, laughing; "but one of the things he said to your credit was, that he was glad you never took advantage of that fact, but did your duty without fear or favour to the last. I hope you've got over your dislike to the old *Flamborough?*"

"Oh yes," replied Mark; "and now that you are like

the Uncle John we had in Bristol, and have dropped the quarter-deck, I'm awfully glad I came; and I know we shall have a jolly time ashore."

"Ha, ha, ha!" laughed Captain Price; "and so I'm different on board ship, am I? a sort of a bear perhaps, eh, boy!"

"Not that exactly," said Mark, getting near the door, "but something very like the ogre in the story you used to frighten us with long ago."

It was almost escaping from our memory to mention that our friend Peter had sailed in the *Flamborough*. At Mark's earnest request, his uncle had taken him as cabin-boy; and now when Mark left the cabin he sought out his friend and communicated to him the good tidings.

"It's all very well for you to say, Ain't it jolly!" said Peter sulkily; "for my part, I wish I'd never listened to you about coming in this here ship."

"Why, Peter, I've heard you say, over and over again, my uncle was the best captain you ever served," replied Mark.

"And suppose I have said that," said Peter, "does it halter the matter? We've been good chums all the cruise; I've taught you a wrinkle or two, you'll not deny, and now you ain't quite so green but what you can pass muster afore that aggrivatin' first-mate. I've told you over and over again he put upon you, and let that lazy lubber Tucker shirk his work afore his very nose. And now that I've got to like you, sort o', here you comes to tell me you're to go ashore, and be made a gentleman of, and go about with the captain; and you'll get so high and mighty that you'll not care to speak a word to the likes o' me, though I'm the best seaman o' the two. I've a good mind to make a bolt of it, and get aboard some foreign craft, and never be heard tell o' more."

"You'll do nothing of the kind," said Mark earnestly. "You don't know what a kind, good-natured man my uncle is ashore; I could bet you a guinea, if I asked him he would take you with us."

"I'll not believe it," said Peter. "He's too much of the gentleman to do it."

When the boat was ready to start on its first trip up to Canton, Peter was of the party, though, strange to say, he appeared more sulky than pleased, and caused Mark to say, as he took his place beside him, "Well, Master Grim-phiz, I wish I hadn't asked you to come."

The river was like a flood of light—well deserving its name of "Pearl"—as they pulled along with the tide; and everything upon or about it was correspondingly wonderful to see, often making it difficult for our hero to keep stroke with his oar. Immense plantations of rice, skirted by bananas and still stranger fruit-trees, extended along the banks; the roots here and there seeming the only thing that kept the water from overflowing its bounds. Pretty little country-houses, of the genuine Chinese pattern, with their sloping, pointed, indented roofs, and their coloured tiles inlaid with different hues, were scattered here and there, under shady trees; while pagodas of various styles raised their heads on little eminences in the neighbourhood of the villages, and

IMPERIAL GARDENS—CHINA.

attracted attention at a great distance. A number of fortifications, looking more like roofless houses than anything else, commanded the bank at various points; and soon the villages followed one another in quick succession, mostly composed of miserable huts, built on piles, driven into the water; while before them lay innumerable boats, which also served as dwellings.

Busier became the scene on the river, and greater the number of ships and inhabited boats. Here were some junks of most extraordinary shape, having poops that hung far over the water, and provided with large windows and galleries, and covered in with a roof like a house. Some of these vessels were of immense size and burthen; but what amused the boys the most was seeing the flat, broad, and long Chinese men-of-war, mounting twenty or thirty cannons.

"Look!" cried Peter, unable to restrain himself longer, even in the captain's presence; "if they haven't gone and got two eyes painted into the prow!"

"Yes, my lad," said the captain good-naturedly; "the Chinese believe that these painted eyes help them to find their way through the water better."

The mandarins' boats, with their painted sides and windows, their carved galleries, and pretty little silk flags, giving them the appearance of the most charming houses, next attracted the attention of the boys. The finest sight of all, however, was the flower-boats, with their upper galleries ornamented with flowers and garlands."

"I should like to get on board of one," replied Mark; "were you ever in one, sir?"

"Oh yes, often," said the captain. "There is a large

apartment divided into cabinets. They adorn the walls with mirrors and silk hangings, and they have glass chandeliers, and coloured paper lanterns, with lovely little baskets of fresh flowers swinging between, which makes them look like fairy palaces."

In addition to these vessels, there were thousands of small boats, some at anchor, some crossing and passing in all directions, with fishermen casting their nets, and men and children amusing themselves by swimming. All this ceaseless activity and never-ending bustle formed such a peculiar feature, that though it was somewhat bewildering, it is needless to say it was highly enjoyed by Mark and his friend Peter.

CHAPTER VII.

CHINA.

AS they passed onwards, another branch of the river would open, lost in a glare of light, amidst glimpses of curious occupations and trades, of which Mark had often heard, and which his uncle promised to let him see by-and-by. At length they were amidst the confusion of the landing-place for the European factories, where the captain went on shore along with the compradore; allowing Mark and Peter also to accompany him. The men, too, had leave by turns to see what they could of the Eastern city, which then alone was accessible to ordinary visitors from the barbarian world, as the Celestials style other countries, however civilized.

Afterwards, along with his uncle, under guidance of Quang Choo, the compradore, Mark had his first stroll through the streets and lanes of Canton, including even a part of the inner town, beyond the fortified states.

Quang Choo was a sharp fellow, who thoroughly understood the sights most worth seeing in Canton. He had not gone far before he said, in his pigeon English, "I say, cappen, you see jeweller's shop. Here's fust-rate shop—number one jeweller, this chap."

"I don't want to see a jeweller's shop particularly," said Captain Price; "I prefer to see the town."

"You no want buy anything for young or old misses at home?" said Quang Choo, with a sly chuckle. "Well, heave along; but young boy want to see, p'raps."

"Well, you may have a peep into one, boys," said the captain; "but mind, look sharp."

There were many beautiful specimens of carving and filigree work in the shop they entered; but what attracted their attention the most was the birds'-feather ornaments, which consisted of gilt or gold head-combs, brooches and ear-rings, on which were firmly fixed with glue strips of the bright blue feathers of the kingfisher, cut into small patterns, through which the gold ground appeared, and having the exact effect of enamelled work. They next went into several porcelain shops, where they saw them not only busily at work in the act of manufacturing the dishes, but engaged in painting them also. Each lad had a small bowl of one colour, and when he had painted in all the parts of the design intended to be of that colour, he passed the plate on to his neighbour, who added his colour; and so on all round the room, where sat ten or twelve lads, till the pattern was completed. They looked so stiff, and the work appeared to be so monotonous, that Peter could not help whispering to

BAKING OF PORCELAIN.

Mark, "After all, I'd rather be afloat than one of them painting chaps; ay, I'd rather be in a stiffish gale even."

After leading them in and out, up and down the narrow streets, or passages rather, of the city, Captain Price could not stand the fatigue any longer, and leaving the two boys to the care of Quang Choo, made off to the river. The day was very sultry, unusually so for that time of the year; and the flagstones were muddy and greasy from rain that had fallen the day before. The air was stagnant, too, from the confinement of closely-packed and overhanging houses, and the swarms of people; and the horrible odour of cabbage-water made the air suffocating. "I tell you what it is, Mark," said Peter, "I'm blowed if I can stand this much longer. I feel sort o' squeamish, for the first time in my life; we must hire one of them sedan-chairs atween us,—or a couple, for that matter."

Mark had no objections, and away they went in search of a sedan-chair, which seemed to be about the last thing to be found when one wanted it in the city of Canton. As they passed along the streets, while Peter kept his eyes wide open for the chair, Mark carefully observed all the buildings worth seeing. He noticed that the houses were narrow-fronted, but extending considerably to the rear. They had no windows, the centre of each front being open; and consisted merely of a carved and painted framework, displaying the contents of the shop on either hand. The back was closed with a large panelling, on which figures of gods, men, animals, and flowers were painted, with a vast deal of gilding and finery. A few of the houses had upper stories, reached by pretty carved balustrade-stairs; and as every article for which space can be found seemed to be hung up for display, both inside the shops and around the front, Mark felt, as he entered the bazaar, as if he were diving into an ocean of cloths, silks, and flags.

All this time Peter had been busily engaged bargaining with a group of sedan-chair bearers, and by the time

Mark and Quang Choo came up, had succeeded in engaging three: one for himself, carried by two bearers—one at either end; another of the same kind for Mark; while Quang Choo, being rather heavy, took his seat in the largest, which was borne by four men.

It was a great relief to emerge from the crowded bazaar, pass through the gateway in the massive city

SEDAN-CHAIR.

wall, and proceed, through comparatively shady lanes, to one or two Chinese gentlemen's houses and gardens, which Quang Choo entered unceremoniously. He also took them, without a word of introduction, to visit one of the temples; and instead of the priests refusing them admittance, they were most courteous. The vergers showed the altars, the various images, the cloisters, and refectories, with great alacrity, extending their hands afterwards for a fee. One of the vergers here stepped forward and offered to sell his finger-nails to the boys. "Well, but if this ain't a curiosity," said Peter; "see, Mark, if this chap's nails ain't four or five inches long!"

"Good for English number one to buy," said the verger; "cappens always buy Chinamen's nails."

"Well, here's a cappen who won't be such a flat," said Peter, turning both his lip and his pug nose up to show his disgust. "They must think a good deal of themselves, with a vengeance."

"I think we have seen enough," said Mark; "I for one, at anyrate, will be very glad to get on board the *Flamborough*."

"And here's number two to that," said Peter, laughing; "so, as we are both agreed, let's be off."

On their way back to the ship that evening they witnessed a very amusing incident. Among the royal methods for raising the supplies in China is that of a certain portion being exacted from the proceeds of the day's work of each labourer, whatever his occupation may be. The mandarins are employed in collecting the imperial dues in their junks on the river; and as the *Flamborough's* boat was passing down, a brisk chase was being given to a small sanpan, the boatman doing everything in his power to escape. At one time he got behind a large ship to avoid being seen, and as soon as the mandarin junk had gone round one way, the boatman in the sanpan would dexterously row off the other. This exciting game went on for some time; but the mandarin junk being armed with long swivel-guns, did not hesitate to throw a shot into the unfortunate sanpan, regardless of the consequences to the boatman.

"Now I call that mean," cried Peter, in a great state of excitement, when the poor boatman was seen struggling to escape from the wreck of his small boat.

"It would have been better had he lain-to," said Mark.

"I don't see that at all," replied Peter. "He deserved to get off for being so plucky."

One afternoon Captain Price took Mark with him to join a party from one of the English man-of-war ships who were going to pay the Chinese one a visit. They found it in a perfect state of confusion, everything uppermost and nothing at hand; and no more respect seemed to be paid to the commander and his officers by the rest of the crew than one sailor pays to another in the forecastle of an English ship, notwithstanding the chief bore the rank of an admiral. They were playing with Chinese cards, and engaged in all sorts of games. Some of the guns were half run-out, some half run-in, and the shot was strewn about the decks in all directions. On this occasion the Chinese deemed it necessary to fire a salute in honour of their distinguished visitors, which consisted of two guns, three being a royal one. It was all the English men-of-war officers could do to keep their gravity to see them fired; and they must have taken more than three minutes to fire them, though they seemed to think they were extra sharp in doing it.

That same afternoon, on Mark's return, he found Peter in close altercation with one of the chopps, whose duty it was to supply the crew with tea hot out of the coppers. The men had set Peter to see that the jars were kept full, and as they emptied them almost as quickly as they were filled, Peter had a pretty hard time of it.

As Mark stepped on board Peter had laid violent hands on the pigtail of one of the unfortunate delinquents, and seeing Mark, he shouted out, "Holloa, shipmate, lend a hand till I dock this here tail short off."

"Oh, save me tail; me get tea plenty!" shouted the unfortunate Chinaman.

"Very well," said Peter magnanimously; "mind you get it better quality too, else I'll not let you off so easily next time."

This lawless proceeding not only produced a more plentiful supply, but of much better quality; and Mark, who now took Peter's place, so that he could watch the Chinese weigher, found his work very easy indeed in consequence. This being the case, he could enjoy watching Peter looking after the weigher. Too-talee-

talee!" cried the Chinaman, meaning in plain English two hundredweights, three quarters, and three pounds; but it often happened that his "too-tallee-tallee" was several pounds short of the weight, and always on the side of the Chinese merchant. There he sat, this Chinese weigher, with a hat a good five feet in diameter; and there stood Peter, his short snub nose peering into the scale—for somehow, as Mark said, Peter seemed to see with his nose—and keeping a sharp look upon the Chinaman. Seeing his mistake, he at once pounced upon him, giving him such a hearty cuff to refresh his memory, as threw the Chinaman, his pigtail, and his hat considerably off their centre of gravity.

"You lubberly son of a Chinawoman," cried Peter, "let me catch you at any more of your cheating, and I'll give you such a docking that your own father won't know you."

"You hold you tongue!" shouted one of the Chinese merchant's clerks, who was seated alongside the capstan, with his desk, stool, pigtail, and finger-nails that might more aptly be called talons from their length. "You one lubber yourself,—number one lubber."

Fortunately one of the mates came on deck at the time, else it was evident the Chinese clerk would have been forced to try the strength of his nails in his own defence.

On the following day Mark went up to town with his uncle, where he witnessed the celebrated Chinese

Feast of Lanterns. From all the houses, at the corners of the roofs, from high posts, from indeed every upright thing, were hung innumerable lanterns, made of paper or gauze, and most artistically ornamented with gods, animals, and warriors. All kinds of refreshments and fruits were laid out, with lights and flowers, in the form

CHINESE FEAST OF LANTERNS.

of half pyramids, on large tables in the courts and gardens of the different houses, and even in the streets themselves. The people wandered about the streets, gardens, and courts until nearly midnight, when the edible portions of the pyramids were eaten by their proprietors; and though the crowds in passing may have looked at the eatables with a scrutinizing glance, not a single fragment was touched. The feast continued through five or six days, during which time at eventide every corner of the city was decorated with streamers and brightly illuminated. Spectators paraded the streets in crowds, letting off crackers, rockets, and squibs, and ingenious fireworks of numberless variety. This feast is intended to show their respect for the spirits of their departed ancestors.

A day or two afterwards, one of the men being ill, the captain sent Mark to the floating apothecary's shop. Mark had been very desirous to see the interior of this strange and novel shop, and very gladly undertook the commission. It was situated a short distance from the shore, and consisted of the hull of an old ship, with three flag-staffs where the masts once stood, having three flags flaunting in the breeze, to indicate the whereabouts of the enterprizing English surgeon. The between-decks was fitted up like a modern surgery or apothecary's shop in London; and he seemed to be getting on in a most flourishing manner, not only among the English shipping, but amongst the Chinese, the better half of whom at Whampoa live upon the water in their sanpans. Mark had a good opportunity of inspecting these close at hand, when he found they had only a covering of mats made of native reeds or bamboo stretched over the sanpans, upon sticks bent like the half of an English hoop. These boats are kept beautifully clean, especially those belonging to the washerwomen, who daily holy-stone them, as sailors do the decks of their vessels, till the interior is as white as the driven snow. Every sanpan is provided with a sail, as well as paddles and oars; the sail consists of a mat, larger or smaller according to the size of the sanpan; in the management of which they are very expert, and can sail at a surprising rate.

When Mark reached the apothecary's floating shop, a number of seamen from all nations were waiting to be served, some evidently there to buy drugs for themselves, others for their shipmates, it might have been; for, judging by the noise they made, it was impossible to suppose they were suffering. Mark got into a corner to wait his turn, and stood watching the busy scene, when a great stir took place outside, and on turning to look out of the port-hole, near which he stood, he discovered that the commotion was caused by the approach of a sanpan with the body of a Chinaman being towed after it attached to a rope. The body had been picked up by the boatman; and as the surgeon had pronounced it lifeless, and no person had come forward to claim it, it was dragged in-shore behind some sedge, to which it was tied by the neck, and there left.

"I'm glad I ain't a Chinaman, I am," said a tall, strong, weather-beaten English sailor, biting off a fresh piece of tobacco. "It's comfortable to think that we get a clean suit, a good piece of sail-cloth to keep out the water, and a shot at our feet to take us safe down."

"Ay, you're right there, shipmate," said another man, with his back to Mark, but whose voice seemed familiar to him. "It's not an agreeable feeling for a man to find his countrymen ain't particular about his body. But see, there are the ducks coming out to it!"

Mark looked in the direction pointed out, and he saw what he had at first taken for a dog-kennel. A flat flooring, he discovered, was placed across a sanpan, over which was erected a roofing, composed of boards slanting upwards from the sides and meeting at the top. The ducks were kept in these erections in flocks of from three to four hundred. The owner or person in charge of the ducks had them under extraordinary training. Upon their being let out, they scrambled for the shore as fast as their feet and wings would carry them, to feed in the swampy places, or in the paddy-fields where the rice grew.

"When he wants to pen them up again," said the sailor, who seemed to take an interest in the ducks especially, "he just whistles, and away they scamper to their sanpan, tumbling over each other to be first in the race; for, you see, the last gets a good whopping for his laziness, though for that matter the poor beast scarcely ever deserves it, seeing they all try hard to be first, and somebody must be last."

All this time the other sailor had been staring hard at our hero, who was too much interested in watching the ducks to pay any attention to him. When he turned round, however, his heart gave a great jump, for, to his astonishment, there stood his old and tried friend Jack Maurice.

"Bless me, boy, how you have growed!" said the worthy Jack, catching hold of Mark's extended hand.

"I can't say you look well," said Mark, "for it's just the very opposite. What have you been doing to yourself to make you look so white and thin?"

"Well I've been ill," replied Jack; "but if I only could get out to the salt ocean once more, I'd be as right and as tight as a man could be. But who's to take me with this white chalky figure-head?"

"Where's your ship you came out in?" said Mark.

"Gone off and left me," said Maurice sulkily; "but mind you, I don't blame any one but this here Jack Maurice's own self. I got on the spree, boy."

"You, Jack!" said Mark in astonishment. "I never knew of you being the worse of drink in my life."

"Ah, but the old fiend once used to be my master; and what's more, he got the better of me once again, though I fancied I had quite cured the demon."

Mark said nothing more, having to make haste back

with the medicine; but as he knew the man who was ill was scarcely expected to recover, he hoped he would be able to induce his uncle to take his old friend Jack Maurice on board when they sailed. Searching his uncle out, he found him beside the sick man, who seemed to be a great deal worse; and when the medicine had been administered, and the man had fallen asleep, the captain returned to the cabin, bidding Mark follow him. "I fear poor Tom is going," he said to Mark. "He is a man I had a great respect for. It will be long before I get another to fill his place."

Here was a very good opportunity to introduce Jack Maurice and his case, and Mark launched out into such an animated description of his good qualities as an able-bodied seaman, that Captain Price, having his "Uncle John's face" on, could do nothing else but agree "to have a look at him." To Mark's great delight, his uncle was pleased with Jack, and though he said with a smile he would have liked had he been "in better condition," it was arranged that Maurice should take up his quarters on board the *Flamborough* at once, as a safeguard against the temptations that beset a sailor's path even in China.

CHAPTER VIII.

HOMEWARD BOUND.

SHORTLY before leaving Whampoa, Peter fell overboard while in the act of drawing a bucket of water. The tide was very strong at the time; but the second-mate, observing a great many Chinese about with their sanpans, did not order a boat to be lowered, as he felt certain the boatmen would pick him up. He was quite mistaken, however; for though they made a dart to pick up the bucket, they left the unfortunate Peter to sink or swim, from a fear, perhaps, of losing caste, or from the strong prejudice they had against Europeans. Peter had been fortunate in seizing hold of a rope fixed in the chains, and though a good swimmer he must soon have been drawn under and drowned, had not the captain, who saw his perilous position from the cabin window, rushed on deck and ordered a boat to be lowered to his rescue just in time to save him.

"You're too bad a penny to lose, Peter," said the mate, as he gave him his hand to help him on deck.

"Thank you kindly, sir," said the incorrigible Peter, determined to take the mate's speech as a compliment. "I'm glad to think I'd ha' been missed from this here craft."

More than one of the men who were standing near laughed outright, for it was well known that there was no love lost between the second-mate and Peter.

Having completed this cargo of tea, the *Flamborough* dropped down clear of the shipping, Quang Choo following in his sanpan, letting off a great many crackers erected on a long pole. This was his parting chin-chin, or thanks for the captain's patronage; an expense he could well afford, according to Mark's idea, from the proceeds of his office, and the way he had contrived to fleece the captain. The Chinese pilot being on board, he took them without accident to the mouth of the Bogue, and three days after they reached Hong-Kong, where they filled up with bales of raw silk, which occupied three or four days more. After thus completing the cargo, they stood for Macao, on the other side of the river's mouth, where they took in some stores for the voyage home. A day or two afterwards, the *Flamborough* tripped her anchor with a fair wind, and set sail for old England.

They were not destined, however, to get quit of the Chinese coast without a sample of the violent weather which often marks those latitudes. The first night there was a heavy banking-up of the clouds, and before morning the *Flamborough* was overtaken by one of the well-known hurricanes peculiar to that region under the name of typhoon. One or two junks were seen labouring against it to reach the land in time to escape, but it was too late for that; and when the white rush of the gale began to attain its height,

A TYPHOON.

there was too much reason to fear that one of the unfortunate junks, at least, fell a victim to the storm. Happily it was not against the course of the English ship; they had been warned by the barometer, so as to reduce canvas before the worst of the gale came, and were thus enabled to weather it out without serious damage. At one point, indeed, towards daybreak, there was a moment when things went very hard with them; the third of three immense seas struck the ship before she could well rise to it, and the volume of water fairly broke along the decks, green and weltering. The caboose on deck was loosened from its fastenings; booms, spars, and boats floated hither and thither; while no one knew whether he had hold of the ship or not. Mark had swallowed more brine than in his whole previous experience; and poor Peter was only stopped by the mizzen-shrouds from being swept overboard, where nothing could have saved him. The ship was on her beam-ends, leaning heavily, as if never to rise; and the captain, helping the men at the wheel, and shouting for axes to cut away a mast, could neither be heard nor obeyed. Providentially the good ship righted herself at last with a convulsive effort, and rose on the billow, streaming water at every outlet; the gale was by this time past the worst; and before long, with additional sail set to steady her, they were heaving away on their course before it.

All went well till she was passing through the Straits

of Banca, between Borneo and the Malayan coasts. The weather was splendid, the breeze favourable, and the worst dangers of the shoals were past; but here they incurred more than one serious risk from the evil designs of the Dayak pirates who infest that vicinity. One set of these made a very cunning attempt to board the *Flamborough* in the night, by means of a trick not uncommon with them, and through which there is reason to think many crews have been murdered. In these straits it is a frequent circumstance to see large portions of turfy soil floating along with the current, covered with long wild grass, and sometimes with the addition of stumps of trees. Jack Maurice, who knew the coast well, and was well acquainted with these pirates, when he discovered that the captain was a comparative stranger to this part of the world, gave him a few hints regarding them. He explained that these portions of floating earth were often imitated by the pirates, by constructing a raft or something like it, capable of holding a number of cut-throats, armed to the teeth; and over whom a covering of this same turfy soil and grass is laid, which is well calculated to deceive strangers. So prepared, Jack explained that those pirates float down upon the vessels in the night, and having succeeded in boarding them, murder the sleeping crew, and plunder the cargo.

A sharp look-out was therefore kept, and by what

followed it proved to be anything but unnecessary. One evening, Jack's quick eyes observed one of those dens of villany quietly dropping down on their starboard-bow, and he immediately reported it to the officer of the watch. Two six-pounders had been kept in readiness for them, besides abundance of small arms; and just as the pirates were dropping quietly into their bow, and within nice reach, a gun was fired to let them see those on board the *Flamborough* were not dozing. They still took no notice, but came gliding down, thinking they would deceive them, and make them think it was indeed nothing but a floating mass of earth. The captain now took more effectual efforts to put them on the right scent. He ordered that the other six-pounder should be fired, which was promptly done, the contents going clean through them. The howling inside could be plainly heard, but by some means they managed to sheer off, and the *Flamborough* saw them no more.

Light winds and calms now rendered the situation of the ship still more dangerous in this respect, and though the treacherous Malays appeared to have received a lesson, yet it proved that this had only forced them to display themselves more decidedly in their true colours. The currents had brought the *Flamborough* unusually near the land, at a point showing signs of more civilized habitation, where caution seemed to be necessary against attack. The chief care now taken was to avoid risk of grounding;

and being at last quite becalmed, the anchor was dropped, and the night came on, leaving all hands wearied with the exertion of the day. Anchor-watch alone was kept, but it proved that fatigue had rendered the men careless, so that they dozed at their posts.

It so happened that Peter, being very thirsty, went up

THE "FLAMBOROUGH" BECALMED.

on deck for a drink of water, when he fancied he heard suppressed voices through the dusk, with the slight plash of oars in the water. He at once gave the alarm, causing the captain to spring on deck; and happily the guns were still loaded, in consequence of the recent attempts upon the ship. They had scarcely time to take their stations, before two or three crowded Malay proas were closing from either side upon the ship; but, being steadily aimed at with the carronades, into several of which extra charges of grape and canister were put, these vessels were soon thrown into disorder. They, in fact, found that the *Flamborough* was much better armed and more numerously manned than they doubtless had supposed. Just at the critical moment, however, all was nearly lost by the addition of another enemy, in the shape of a small sailboat which had been lying in there, as if quietly taking advantage of the anchorage. This vessel, which turned out to be a so-called native trader, must have thought to take advantage of the *Flamborough's* position by helping the pirates; and they now made a stealthy attempt to board over the stern, where danger was not looked for. Mark was the first to perceive the new peril. He fired a ship's pistol at the aggressors, thus bringing some of the men to his help; the result being that they were driven down with loss. Meanwhile the Malays in the proas gave way, and drew off discomfited; and as a breeze began to ruffle the water, enabling the ship to lift her anchor and gain open water, she was now in a position to defy further attack. Alarm had been caused on shore, where the people of the village were obliged to appear friendly to European vessels, well knowing the power of Rajah Brooke with his steam-cruisers in the Straits.

In the act of repelling this attack, our hero, Mark, had got what he thought a mere prick in the leg from an arrow, shot by the native crew of the sail-boat, being one amongst several which were aimed at the deck. It gave him but little pain at first, and he was thinking no more about it, when one of the men asked another how it had been fired.

"He blowed it out of his mouth through a cane," said Bill Hooper.

"Then I'm blessed if it wasn't one o' their sumpitans," replied Jack Maurice. "It's poisoned! It's deadly, it is."

"He's a dead man," said another sailor; "it's the rank upas-venom—there's no 'arthly cure for't."

Mark turned pale, and naturally thought his last morning had come, when he saw the streaks of dawn breaking before them in the east.

Captain Price, however, when he came aft, looked upon the matter not quite so desperately. He knew more of the Malay poisons than most men, and said that when the arrows had been some time dipped, as was most likely the case, they lost much of their virulence; and instantly applied sulphuric acid and caustic. While he was doing this, Jack Maurice came in to see how he was getting on; for it may be supposed his former friendship for the lad when aboard the *Stratton* had ripened into sincere affection.

"Come, old ship," said the captain good-naturedly, in reply to Maurice's respectful inquiry, "you must give us none of your long faces here; the lad will be all right in a trice. I am of opinion he will feel no bad effects whatever."

"I hope so, sir," said Maurice. "I've had some experience of them Malays, and I know they don't believe their poison is altogether deadly, though the Kayans believe it."

"Have you seen their arrows, Jack?" said Mark.

"Oh yes, often," replied Maurice. "They carry them about in a bamboo case hung at the side, and at the bottom of the quiver is the poison of the upas. The arrow is a piece of wood sharp-pointed, and put into a socket, made of the pith of a tree, which fits the tube of the blow-pipe. The natives carry a small calabash for these arrow-heads, and on going into action prepare a number, and dip the points in the poison, as its deadly power does not continue long."

"I have heard so too," said the captain; "and my belief is, that as we came so very unexpectedly, they would only have old ones with them. I have been told they fire them very dexterously."

"Yes, sir; I believe they do," said Maurice. "When they face an enemy the box at the side is open, and whether advancing or retreating they fire fast and aim well. Some hold four spare arrows between the fingers of the hand which grasps the sumpitan, but most of them take their side-case."

"You seem to know a great deal about them, Maurice," said the captain. "How is that?"

"I was taken prisoner once, sir, and had to serve aboard one of them proas for ever so long; and a hard time I had of it till I made my escape."

"But how do they fire the arrows from their mouth?" inquired Mark.

"In advancing, the sumpitan is carried at the mouth, and sloping upwards, which they fire by the force of their breath."

"To what distance will the arrows go?" inquired the captain.

"To a distance of twenty yards with certainty, sir," replied Maurice. "Beyond that their aim is not steady, from the lightness of the arrow; but on a calm day the range may be a hundred yards."

When the captain was left alone with Mark, after Jack Maurice had left the cabin, he said to his nephew, "I like your friend Jack very much; he seems to be a very intelligent man, and it is my impression he must have seen better days. I mean by that, that he converses as if he had been well educated, and might hold a better position than a common sailor."

"Oh yes, uncle," said Mark, "I am quite sure Jack must have been a gentleman born. I know once he spoke to me, when we were in the *Stratton*, of his college days; but he seemed to be vexed he had done it, and he always was very close about his friends."

"Well, as we may say he has in a manner saved the ship from these bloodthirsty cut-throats, we must see what can be done for him with the owners."

Whether Mark had received any poison in the arrow-wound or not cannot be said; but he became so listless, that all his usual flow of spirits and animation seemed to have left him. The captain and Jack Maurice did their utmost to cheer him, but without effect; and poor Peter, who now became as a dog in faithfulness to his friend, played off his merriest pranks, but could not succeed in drawing out the faintest smile. As they were likely to be short of that most important part of a ship's stores, water, the captain decided upon touching at St. Helena. He was the more desirous to do this that he might get advice for Mark. As they drew near the island Mark recovered somewhat, and showed some interest, and seemed even pleased to get a view of it. As they sailed round the point and caught a sight of the large but plain-looking whitewashed house, the former residence of Bonaparte, and the garrison for the troops, overlooking the sea, Mark appeared almost his old self again. While the water was being got on board, the captain desired Jack to take Mark and Peter on shore to the doctor's house. After he had prescribed for him, they had a good walk through James's Town, the principal place in the island, lying near the foot of Ladder Hill, on the top of which the barracks are built. They were much interested in seeing the strong fortifications, and the battery of large guns, slung in chains on the top, a shot from any of which must crush through an enemy's ship with fearful effect. On their return to the harbour, a ship came in with one of the sailors on board in a dreadful state from scurvy. The people on shore resorted to a singular means for his cure. This consisted in burying his legs in the earth in a newly-dug hole, where he was to be kept for four hours; but as the *Flamborough* was to leave in a very short time, they had no means of discovering if he was really cured or not.

Though Mark had in a measure appeared to be improving after leaving St. Helena, he fell back into the same listless state he was in before — even into a worse state. The captain was very glad when they entered the British Channel, and after a time got their pilot on board. It happened to be the same one who had taken the *Stratton* down when Mark first went to sea. And now he discovered that under a rough coat and gruff voice and manner could be hidden a very kind heart.

"Why, what's come over ye, boy?" he said, when Mark came on deck, his legs scarcely able to carry him. "I think I mind o' seeing ye go out as hearty a lad as need be; and, if I recollect right, I gave ye your first

MARK'S OLD FRIEND.

touch of sea discipline. Didn't I mast-head you, or some'at?"

"You sent me aloft, at anyrate," said Mark, smiling faintly, "before I had my sea-legs on; but I was all the better of it."

"In course," said the pilot, with a merry twinkling of his weather eye; "and what you want now is a little coddling; but mammy at home will do that in style. Shouldn't wonder, now, but what she goes and overdoes it, and you turns out a land-lubber in the end."

Mark was about to make some indignant response to this latter statement, but somehow the mention of his mother's name had upset him. He felt his heart give a bound when he thought of how she would receive him, and how she would coddle him, as the pilot called it, and his whole soul went out towards her; and, being in such a weak state at anyrate, he fairly broke down, and, in spite of the rough pilot's presence, cried like a girl.

"What's this you've been a-doing or a-saying to Mark Willis?" said Peter, who came up at the moment. "I'd fight ye, ye sea-lion, if ye had two fins to fight with; but as you han't, ye are sort o' protected."

Instead of being angry at Peter's impertinent remark, the rough pilot was the very opposite; and when the boat was got out for the captain to take Mark home, he insisted upon him leaning upon his arm. "It's only the left one, but it's next the heart," he said, which remark made Peter, who was standing by, quite penitent, and he exclaimed under his breath, "He's a good un, he is!"

In a short time Mark was at home, lying snugly on his mother's little couch by the side of a blazing fire, and feeling that every wish of his heart was gratified. "If I could only see Father Fritz, mother," he had said, "my happiness would be complete;" and of course one of the boys was instantly despatched to fetch him. As Mr. Fritz said afterwards, he verily believed, had he refused to come, he would have been carried off by main force. Indeed, Mark's two brothers were not only devoted to Mark, they were his veriest slaves. He was in their eyes a hero indeed; for had he not shot "a savage pirate," and been wounded in a sea-fight, and behaved himself like one of the famous people in history?

It was days before Mark was strong enough to go to the cathedral; but it came at last, and Mr. Fritz played some of his very finest music, that brought the tears rolling up into the sick boy's eyes, for he knew his old friend was playing with his whole heart and soul, sending up a song of thanksgiving for the safe return of the lad, and for his recovery. No one spoke of the sea any more. Kind-hearted Uncle John set sail once more in the *Flamborough* for a distant port; and though Mark heard all about it, he appeared to take no interest at the time, and his mother's heart was glad. But after that day in the cathedral Mark began to recover rapidly, and would wander away to the old favourite seat in the college green, within sound of the organ, and dream again of being at sea and coming home a captain. The sea-breezes seemed to strengthen him; and every returning day his wish to be afloat again grew stronger and stronger, till Mrs. Willis saw there was no use to struggle against it. The hammock and sea-chest were got out once more, and Mark sailed away as happy as if this had been his first voyage, and as eager as ever to behold the strange sights in distant lands.

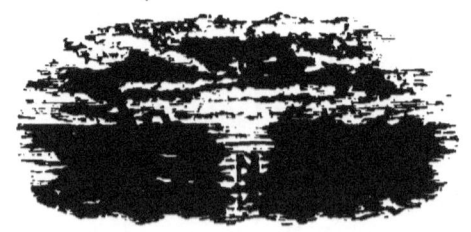

www.ingramcontent.com/pod-product-compliance
Lightning Source LLC
Chambersburg PA
CBHW030248170426
43202CB00009B/671